THE PROS

*A Documentary
of Professional Football
in America*

by ROBERT RIGER

commentary by
TEX MAULE

SIMON AND SCHUSTER
NEW YORK
1960

DESIGNED BY ROBERT RIGER

LIBRARY OF CONGRESS CATALOG CARD NUMBER: 60-14284
ISBN: 978-1-5011-4761-6
GRAVURE TEXT PRINTED IN MILAN, ITALY, BY AMILCARE PIZZI
UNDER THE SUPERVISION OF CHANTICLEER PRESS, NEW YORK
GRAVURE JACKET, FRONTISPIECE AND ENDPAPERS PRINTED BY THE BECK ENGRAVING CO., PHILADELPHIA
LITHOGRAPHY BY THE WRIGHT LITHOGRAPHING CO., INC., NEW YORK
BOUND BY H. WOLFF, NEW YORK

CONTENTS

INTRODUCTION

ONE OF THE luckiest breaks I have ever had as a sports artist came in 1950, when the New York Giants gave me permission to work from the sidelines during their games. I wanted to see the action as the players saw it; the sketches on these pages were made on the field that first October afternoon ten years ago. But I found that in a sketchbook you can record only the quiet moments of a game. The complex, shifting panorama of football cannot be drawn by looking up from a pad. I wanted to be accurate and precise, but the eye alone cannot retain the complete image of each play. So the next week I took a camera, and even the first pictures proved amazing in the information they revealed. As the years passed I began to stockpile a great wealth of material on pro football, my favorite sport.

My real good fortune came, however, in 1954, when *Sports Illustrated* began publication. I joined the magazine as a free-lance artist in the first month, and my initial assignment was on pro football. The material I had accumulated during the chilly Sundays at the Polo Grounds was, and remains, wonderfully useful.

In nine years, I have used ten different cameras to build up my file of football pictures. These photographs are my source material for game reports and drawings. The more than 200 photographs in this book are a small part of that file and have never been published before.

I have always been fascinated by the detail and design of football play, and the camera helps me catch it all and leave the stadium with the ballgame in my pocket. I can take a split second's action and quietly dissect it a day or a year later. This is when

I find out how the players looked and played, and from this documentation I do my drawings. The reader demands accuracy, and as an artist-reporter this has been the cornerstone of my success.

I began to follow pro football in 1935 because I liked Dutch Clark. I liked the way he looked and played, and I read all I could find about him. As a boy I lived on Coogan's Bluff over the Polo Grounds and I watched all the Giant games either from the rocks high above the stands or from a bleacher seat. From the end zone I saw the pattern of play, the deception and blocking, and this perspective became football to me. The memory of the great players of the Thirties and their rugged rivalries played a great part in my decision to be a sports artist. There were a handful  of sports artists in the country after the war but all of these were cartoonists for newspapers. I thought I could make a living by drawing sports with realism. Today I have the rare privilege of earning my entire living from sports pictures.

FOOTBALL is not an easy game to photograph. Its momentum, diversity, and complexity are confusing and difficult to interpret in a clear manner. You cannot photograph it well unless you know a great deal about the techniques of football, the teams playing, and the players. You never have a second chance at a picture in football. No one poses for you. The action flows by and is gone, and it never happens just that way again. You never watch a football game or you'll miss the picture. You just keep the camera on the ball and this is tremendously exciting. You need an inexhaustible supply of film and energy and you must go out every Sun-

day and follow every play so you'll have that touch and be ready for that key game assignment.

THE IMPACT of my pictures is heightened by putting the reader right up in there—alongside 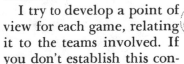 the great quarterback about to pass—over the shoulder of the end about to catch one—opposite the stare of the line-backer.

I try to develop a point of view for each game, relating it to the teams involved. If you don't establish this continuity your photographs are likely to be accidental, fragmentary, and meaningless. When I take a photograph I am making an illustration, a representative picture of that game and of all football too. As in art, the photograph must extend beyond the actual fact.

Every artist should have a concept of life. If it is universal and clear and intensified by a personal style, the art is good—maybe even significant. My concept is dramatic, my style is the documentary. My subject is sports. It gives me an honest world to document dramatically.

However, a picture, no matter how good, is not really worth a thousand words. In a newspaper or a magazine or a book it is worth very little without the proper words to complement it.

Tex Maule is an excellent writer and one of the nation's real football experts. His commentary in this book is invaluable. We have worked together on many successful assignments for *Sports Illustrated* and we hope that if you like football as well as we do you will enjoy seeing the pros as we see them—as they truly are.

ROBERT RIGER

PREFACE

HE WAS a potbellied little man with a frog voice and he knew more about football than anyone. He played it and coached it and he was president of the National Football League and, a small man in a world of giants, he did very well. He died at a professional football game, and I guess that if you had asked Bert Bell the way he wanted to go, he would have said, "At a pro football game."

Death came for him at a game between the Philadelphia Eagles and the Pittsburgh Steelers last year, and the stands were full, which must have made him very happy. As much as any one man, he was responsible for the filled stands. Pete Rozelle, the new commissioner, is a young, able and personable man, well grounded in pro football and eminently fit to carry out Bell's plans and inaugurate programs of his own.

Bert came from a very posh Philadelphia family. There were society and politics and wealth, and Bert must have seemed a throwback to an earlier, lustier time. He went to the University of Pennsylvania and played football there, and later he coached the team. Back in the early Thirties, he bought the moribund Philadelphia Eagles and they remained moribund under his direction. Bert coached the team reasonably well, but you can't win without the horses and he didn't have horses. And he was involved in all the other myriad details of running a professional football team, too. Once he stood on a downtown street corner in Philadelphia and hawked tickets to the Eagle games. He found very few takers. The nadir of his career as a pro football owner came at one game when there were more inhabitants of the press box than there were spectators in the stands.

Maybe Bert's trouble was that he was ahead of his time. He was elected commissioner of the National Football League on January 11, 1946. At the time, he was a part owner of the Pittsburgh Steelers, and more than a few of the owners thought they were electing a figurehead. Bert changed their minds in a hurry.

He never took a step back from anyone, least of all the owners. In the frequent and bitter arguments between owner and owner, and owner and player, Bert was always fair. It was Bell who designed and implemented the league policy on television, which made pro football the fastest-growing professional sport in the United States. It was this little, fat and stubborn man who introduced the player draft to pro football and so equalized the teams in the league that on any Sunday the lowest team can, with a break, beat the best.

None of that really makes any difference. Bert was a strong man and an intelligent one, and, above all, a fair man. You could call him at three o'clock in the morning—as I did once or twice—and he would talk to you without resentment or anger, and in the last few years that took self-control because he was a sick man. His heart had begun to fail, but he overlooked that, as he overlooked anything which might have made him less of a commissioner.

I talked to him for a long time one afternoon just a couple of weeks before he died. Our conversation was interrupted by phone calls from owners and players, and in one of these calls he told an owner he was a cheapskate for trying to avoid paying an injured player.

Then he turned to me and said, "Tex, the one thing we can't forget is that this game was built and made popular by the players. We owe them everything. I don't think that any group of athletes in the world can match pro football players for honesty and character and strength."

He was, of course, right.

TEX MAULE

Part One

THE OLD PROS *1920-1950*

IT BEGAN in a decade of restlessness and answered a need for violence. The Twenties, like the Fifties, were turbulent years, and it is no accident that professional football was born from that turbulence. Young men fresh from the wars needed a socially acceptable outlet for their emotions; too old for college and impatient of campus restrictions, a few of them turned to pro football as players, and, as the decade grew older, more and more of them found a vicarious release from tension as spectators.

In the small towns of America, the pro teams sprang up, flourished briefly and died. But in one, the team survived and survives now. Green Bay is the oldest town in Wisconsin. In the Twenties, it was inhabited by some 31,000 people; pro football had existed sporadically for twenty years in Green

Bay by then. When Curly Lambeau organized the Packers, he had a small nucleus of fans to draw from, but it was Lambeau's persistence which kept the team alive. Curly, the son of a Belgian building contractor, organized the team with $500 put up by a packing company. For a few years the club played at Hagemeister Park, a ramshackle structure near a brewery of the same name. There were no fences and no tickets; the players passed a hat after the game, and, at the end of the 1919 season, the share of each player came to $16.75. But the club survived, and in the violent climate of the decade it began to prosper.

In 1925, the team moved into the new City Stadium. Now tickets were printed and sold and the team was in the National Football League, but Lambeau was still the owner, coach and star. In

the next few years, more stars came: men like John McNally, a wild young man who left the Notre Dame campus in search of excitement and found it as Johnny Blood. He picked Blood as a name from the marquee of a theater advertising a motion picture called *Blood and Sand*. The star was Rudolph Valentino. Johnny, "the vagabond halfback," was ringleader on the championship teams of 1929-30-31.

Curly Lambeau, Johnny Blood, Red Grange, Cal Hubbard, Jugger Earp, Benny Friedman, George (The Brute) Trafton—the restless young men came in a steady stream and they played for the Bears and the Packers and the Giants and they answered the need of a violent generation. They built pro football so that it survived until another violent generation—the postwar generation of the Fifties—could make it a mushrooming success.

This is Curly Lambeau, advertising a meat-packing company. Pro football started this way—with Lambeau and the other pioneers.

The Legend of Jim Thorpe

A MOODY, CHILDLIKE Sac and Fox Indian was very likely the greatest all-around athlete in the history of sport. The years and the magnifying glass of memory have made him bigger than he was. When old-timers like George Halas of the Bears, or Greasy Neale, who coached the Eagles, talk about Jim Thorpe, they call him Big Jim and you get the idea that he was a giant of a man. By modern standards, he was almost too small to play on a pro club. He stood an even six feet and weighed 175 pounds; maybe his accomplishments made him seem bigger. He came off a reservation to play football with the Carlisle Indians and he scored twenty-five touchdowns one season. He could punt seventy-five yards and pass or catch passes. He could drop-kick fifty yards or place-kick as far, and, above all, he could run. He could, quite literally, do everything. He won both the pentathlon and the decathlon in the 1912 Olympics; no one had ever done that before and no one has done it since. He was a fine baseball player too, playing right field for the Giants in the 1913 World Series.

Football was his favorite sport. His grandfather had been a warrior and in Jim the savage love of warfare was only thinly covered over by a gloss of civilization. He had a cold, stoic Indian face and he had at best a rudimentary conception of the white man's definition of right and wrong. His career as a pro lasted from 1913 to 1925, and he was, oddly enough, the first president of the American Football League, predecessor to the National Football League.

He began playing professionally with a team in Pine Valley, Pennsylvania, and he finished, tired and old, with the New York Giants. In between he played with the Canton Bulldogs and with a team of his own which represented a kennel club and was called the Oorang Indians, after the kennel. In twelve years, on the strength of his name and his ability, he had as much to do as any one man in keeping pro football alive, and he created a hundred legends, some of which are true.

He played with or against all the great players of his generation and he overshadowed most of

Jim Thorpe will never be forgotten by the men who played against him. Here is the way he looked in the Canton Bulldog uniform.

12

them. Steve Owen, a great tackle in his playing days, met Thorpe in 1923, in the twilight of the Indian's career. Thorpe was playing for a team called the Toledo Maroons, and Owen, a strong young man just out of college, was playing for the Oklahoma All-Stars. Twice he ran over Jim to tackle a Toledo ball carrier and he told the guard beside him, "Old Jim's slowed up. He doesn't like to block any more." On the next play, Thorpe hit Owen with a violent, battering block and when the big youngster got up the aging Thorpe, his Indian face impassive, said softly, "Always keep an eye on the old Indian, son."

Jim played against the Nesser brothers and Knute Rockne and Gus Dorais and Greasy Neale and George Halas, and game by game he built the legend of the old Indian. He was a violent, sometimes cruel, player with an Indian's disregard for pain, either to himself or to the victims of his violence. He played with his shoulder pads stiffened by sheet iron; when tackling from behind, he threw a high cross body block in the small of the runner's back. He was not perfect; there were days when he played lackadaisically. He had an Indian's weak-

ness for liquor and an Indian's inability to hold it. It was probably after a drinking bout that he contributed to one of the oldest records in pro football, George Halas' 98-yard return of a fumble for a touchdown. Halas, owner, coach and end of the Chicago Bears, was playing against Jim's own team, the Oorang Indians. Jim fumbled going in for a touchdown on the Bear two, and George, with the old Indian in full pursuit, raced 98 yards with the ball. "I never ran faster in my life," he says now, as he thinks back to that Sunday long, long ago. "I could feel Big Jim in the small of my back all the way."

Big Jim was the symbol and the perfect expression of an era. His career ended ingloriously with the New York Giants and, fittingly, his last year was the first of the era of Grange. With the coming of Red Grange, pro football left its rough-and-tumble haphazard days and began, surely, to become the big business it is today.

Jim would have been out of place in the modern game. He was too small and too wild. But pro football will remain forever in his debt, and he will remain forever in pro football as a legend.

The Beginning of the League

THE National Football League was born in the showroom of an automobile agency in Canton, Ohio, on a hot summer night in September 1920. Of the dozen men who sat and sweated and planned in that long-ago time when the automobiles had running boards for them to sit on, only one is still active in the league. He is George Halas, then and now owner of a team which played as the Decatur Staleys in 1920, and has played for forty years as the Chicago Bears.

Halas was the most prescient of that small group of men who somewhat grandiosely decided that the small towns in Pennsylvania and Ohio and Illinois which had pro football clubs should be dignified with the name of the American Professional Football League. Not long after that, they changed the league title to the National Football League. They priced franchises at $100, and not many of them had $100 in cash. Actually, you could buy a franchise in the NFL for the promise to field a team; today a franchise is worth between two and three million dollars.

Pro football competition was formalized with

the young league. Reasonably firm scheduling replaced the haphazard arrangements for games which had prevailed earlier. There were still wildcat teams in other sections of the nation, but, for the first time, the champion of the National Football League could truly claim to be the world champion. As the league scrabbled desperately for a toehold on the national sports scene, the small towns gradually dropped out of the picture and the franchises were shifted to New York and Chicago and Cleveland and Philadelphia, where bigger crowds could pay the increasing costs of supporting a pro team.

As the big cities accepted the teams and the sport began to burgeon, the men who had sat and dreamed on the running boards in 1920 disappeared from the scene. The actuality had far outstripped their dreams; the little man with a small bankroll became as much of an anachronism in pro football as the running board on an automobile. But theirs was the vision and the courage, and to them must go the honor of creating America's most exciting spectacle.

Red Grange and the Bears

RED GRANGE was a little man with a wonderful talent for evading people. In his three varsity years at the University of Illinois, he created a legend in American football which has persisted until today. When he turned pro in 1925, he gave this new and dynamic sport a lift which carried it from the backlots of the small towns of the nation into the big stadia and the big cities. No one man, other than Bert Bell, is more responsible for the growth of pro football than Red Grange.

He came into pro football as the early era was dying out. The Canton Bulldogs and the Massillon Tigers had served their purpose and were only warm memories. The sport had moved into the big

George Halas, in 1922

cities — Chicago and New York and Philadelphia and Pittsburgh—and it needed new blood and new faces to fill the big parks. In 1925, Red Grange, the Wheaton Iceman, was Mr. Football. His name —like Babe Ruth's and Bobby Jones's and Jack Dempsey's—was pure magic, and no one knew that better than George Halas, who owned the Chicago Bears. George was a young man then—intense and strong and intelligent — and he believed wholeheartedly in professional football. He knew that his team needed a box-office name; there was no better name then than Red Grange, and George set out to acquire that name. Unfortunately, a small-town promoter named C. C. (for Cash and Carry) Pyle had signed Grange to a personal service contract and Halas had to pay dearly. "I figured a one-third cut of the gate was about right," Halas said. "We agreed on the percentage. But Pyle wanted two thirds, leaving the Bears the one third."

The deal was made, eventually, and the Bears took off on a killing tour to capitalize on the name of Grange. They played eight games in twelve days, and Grange and Pyle made a hundred thousand dollars apiece out of the tour. The Bears did well enough, too, but the big winner was professional football, which, for the first time, drew national headlines. The tour, in some ways, was prophetic of things to come. The Bears played the Giants in New York and drew over 65,000 people (so many stormed the gate that an accurate count was impossible) and put the Giants on their feet financially. Pro football came of age with Grange. It might eventually have come of age anyway, but the dramatic impact of this one small, talented halfback gave it an invaluable boost.

Pro football had moved up in class; the days of the Thorpes and the Nessers and the wild men were over and the pros had achieved respectability. No longer would it be necessary for a campus star to play under an assumed name; Grange had changed all that.

THE BEARS benefited enormously. Red Grange gave Halas' club a cachet which for years made it easy for Halas to corral the biggest and strongest and best of the college crop—until Bert Bell introduced the draft system, or "equalization," as he called it, giving the last-place team first choice of the best players. But in the meantime, the Bears had a bull of a man from Minnesota named Bronko Nagurski, a wild, violent end named George Wilson and a host of other players who created the image of the Monsters of the Midway.

These early Bears revised the game for Grange's option pass and Nagurski's jump pass changed the face of football. For the first time, the true attacking weapon was through the air; both Grange and Nagurski could run wonderfully well, but, if they passed and hit, the defense gave up a touchdown instead of a considerable gain. All the runner-passers since that time have traded on the Grange-Nagurski threat—the Frank Giffords and the Glenn Davises and the Doak Walkers. They do it a little better than the old redhead or the big buster from the Midwest—but they owe it to Grange and Nagurski and an old Bohemian—in race, not in habit—named Halas. For it was Halas who recognized the diabolical choice the option off a sweep or a plunge offered the defense—damned if you do and damned if you don't. No fullback since Nagurski has used the pass off a power play as well; many halfbacks are as good as Grange. But they changed the game.

The Pass off the End Run

Here's Grange swinging wide, arm cocked as if to throw. The defense had an impossible problem—come up fast to stop Red's run or hold off to stop his pass? There was no correct answer—and on this the Bears predicated some great teams. One man—Grange—made the difference.

GRANGE retired in 1933. At the league meeting that year, Halas and Marshall lobbied for two rules changes which were to make pro football the spectacular game it is today. First, they pushed through a rule that a pass could be thrown from anywhere behind the line of scrimmage. Previously, the rule said that the passer must be at least five yards back of the scrimmage line. Second, they passed a rule that the goal posts should be placed on the goal line instead of ten yards behind it. These two changes opened up the game tremendously. It may not have been an accident that Halas wanted the passing rule changed or that Marshall agreed with him.

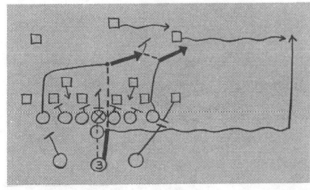

In Bronko Nagurski, Halas had a pulverizing fullback who could shrink any defense by feinting a run up the middle, then take advantage of the suddenly closed-up defenders by throwing over them. (Above, right)

15

This was Sammy Baugh —a lean, leather-tough gentleman from Texas who could throw a football better than any man who had ever lived before him. He was cool and strong and ornery and he lasted longer than any player in the history of the pros.

Baugh passing was not really a picture thrower. The old cliché about passing is that the quarterback throws the ball off his ear, with a straight-ahead motion. Actually, none of the great ones threw that way. Look at Sam here and you'll see that the throwing motion is more sidearm— and, of course, deadly straight. (Below: his favorite plays)

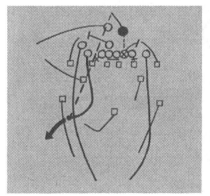
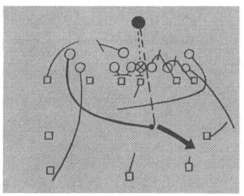
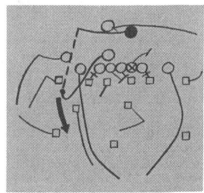

The Passer from Texas

SAM ADRIAN BAUGH was tall and thin and he looked like a cowboy. He had been a great football player at Texas Christian University and, at the time, he threw a football better than anyone had ever thrown one before. He was signed by the Washington Redskins, and when George Preston Marshall, the owner of the Redskins, called him, he was not surprised.

"Buy some cowboy boots and a ten-gallon hat," Marshall said and Sam smiled.

"What size you wear?" he asked Marshall.

"What difference does that make?" Marshall said. "They're for you."

"Never wore boots and a big hat in my life," said Baugh, and he was right. But the image of Baugh in Marshall's mind created a new Baugh, as very often happens. Baugh began to fit the picture of a tall, bowlegged Texan who lived on a horse. He got off the plane in Washington wearing a ten-gallon hat and cowboy boots and he was the greatest passer who ever came down the pike. There have been better ones since, but you have to remember the time and the man and the time was the late thirties and the man was a cold, nerveless Texan who could do everything a football player should do. He could run well enough on thin, pipe-stem legs and he could punt superbly and, above everything else, he could pass incomparably.

He began learning to throw a football as a kid. He used to spend hours throwing at an automobile tire swinging on a rope from a tree branch, and eventually he could throw a football through the tire while he was running.

Football, at that time, had only just graduated from a strictly running game. In the Southwest Conference, Matty Bell had an aerial circus at Southern Methodist University, and Dutch Meyer, the coach at Texas Christian, had begun to copy it. In the final game of the season, SMU beat TCU for the Southwest Conference championship on a Bobby Wilson pass. But Baugh was the better passer, and Marshall, an eagle-nosed, Indian-faced man who had a deep and abiding belief in pro football, recognized Baugh as the savior of the sport in Washington, D. C.

You have to remember the two men as they were then. Marshall, who had been a very successful laundry operator, was fighting for survival. He had tried in Boston and failed and moved to Washington, and he needed a single dynamic player to sell pro football. He saw that player in Baugh, and when he called Sammy and asked him to buy a ten-gallon hat and boots, he was insuring Baugh's appeal to his fans.

In the next sixteen years, Sam grew accustomed to his boots. He also grew accustomed to playing pro football, and under his leadership, the Washington Redskins came into their own. Baugh, when he first came up, was a tailback. After the Chicago Bears whipped the Redskins 73-0 in a championship game which made the T formation popular, he became a T quarterback. He didn't like the new role at first, but after he had made the switch, he said, "In this formation I can play in a top hat and tails, man." He could have, too. The Redskins protected him marvelously. Baugh and Sid Luckman of the Bears became the prototypes of the modern T quarterback—of Unitas and Graham and the rest. Because of their ability to fake and pass and, rarely, run, pro football became—and remained—explosive game. Sammy owns a ranch near Rotan, Texas, now, and he has become, at last, a cowboy.

Complement to Baugh's passes was the running of Cliff Battles, a hard-nosed, tough and indefatigable ball carrier. "He could do everything," Sammy said, "better than anybody." And that was true for a very long time for Battles.

The Giants...

A DIGNIFIED, gray-haired gentleman who was an honest bookmaker with a sharp eye for a good bet bought a franchise in New York from the National Football League in 1925 because the asking price was only $250. "Son," Timothy J. Mara said as he wrote the check, "any New York franchise is worth that much."

It proved to be worth much more. Mara at that time was only hazily aware that a football is an oblate spheroid, but he had an intense pride and a driving desire to succeed, and eventually he put together what has been, over the years, probably the most successful franchise in the league. The Giants have, of course, had bad years; but their bad years have been rare and their good years many and the heroes who have worn a Giant uniform are legion.

Red Grange, playing with the Chicago Bears, put the Giants comfortably in the black by drawing some 65,000 people to the Polo Grounds. But Mara's astute player-procurement program kept them there; he acquired a succession of the finest players who ever performed and they brought him more than a fair share of championships—and fame. Early in the life of the Giants, Mara hired a husky young man from Oklahoma, first as a player, then as a coach. Steve Owen was a worthwhile investment; he became, over the years, the shrewdest defensive coach in professional football. Steve, like Greasy Neale of the Eagles, was above all else a realist. "Coaching is easy," he said once. "Just get the horses."

Mara got the horses and Steve polished them and the Giant dynasty, which is still in progress, has dominated Eastern professional football most of the time since. From 1927, the Giants have played for a record eleven championships, won four. They have nearly always been in contention.

Going back to the early days of the Giants, you pick up legendary names in pro football. There was Mel Hein, a big, black-haired center from the Northwest who was a nearly perfect linebacker.

"He was easy to coach," said Owen. "Mel didn't need coaching. He knew more about it than I did." Hein, moving mstinctively behind the very good Giant lines, was an unerring tackler. He moved with startling speed for his size, and he was probably first to make the knowledgeable fans of the New York Giants aware of the importance of defense.

But he was only one of the many Giant stars who have marched across the decades. There was Ken Strong, a New York boy, who was a tremendous punter, a wonderful runner and a crushing blocker. Alphonse Leemans was a fiery competitor who earned his nickname ("Tuffy") by the aggressiveness of his play, and Ward Cuff matched him in speed and power and general hell-for-leather meanness. The first time Tuffy—an unheralded back from George Washington University—carried the ball as a Giant, he ran forty-five yards for a touchdown. Cuff played almost unnoticed in a Marquette University backfield which had the famous Buzz Buivid and the Gueppe brothers in it. He learned to run and kick for the Giants and he could always block; that's why Owen picked him.

The Giant tradition has been carried on under an old Owen end—Jim Lee Howell. It's safe to say that it will go on under Mara's sons, too. Jack and Wellington Mara have an advantage over their father: they came into the sport knowing the shape of a football.

Here's Ken Strong doing what he could do best—kicking. With his kicking and running he scored 351 points in his 8 years with the Giants.

18

The Revolutionary T Formation

IN THE DAWN of football, someone thought of the T formation and everybody used it. It was the natural way to line up to put the ball in play. But, obviously enough, the defense caught up with the T quickly. Then for a long while no one used the T. They used Knute Rockne's Notre Dame box or the single wing, and only one stubborn man in Chicago stuck with the old-fashioned T.

He was George Halas. The Bears did well enough with the T—not spectacularly well but at least respectably. Then they fell on evil times for a few years and Halas decided the T needed refurbishing. He brought in Ralph Jones from little Delaware College and Clark Shaughnessy, who was struggling to keep feeble University of Chicago, with no players to speak of, alive in the Big Ten. These were two of the most inventive minds in football; they rebuilt and redesigned the T, adding the man-in-motion and a counterplay against the flow of man-in-motion—a play which struck away from the reaction of the defense. In 1940, the Chicago Bears demolished the Washington Redskins, 73-0, to win the championship, and the T formation was reborn. The pro attacks began to explode and the fans loved it. (See diagram below.) Shaughnessy, meanwhile, had gone on to coach Stanford, and undefeated Stanford won the Rose Bowl title, again with the T.

THE MEN who implemented this new attack were great football players. Sid Luckman, a quarterback from Columbia University via Erasmus Hall High in Brooklyn, devoted endless hours under Shaughnessy's tutelage to learning the intricate ballet work of the T fakes. At first, Nagurski was the fullback, then came Bill Osmanski. George McAfee was a will-o'-the-wisp halfback, and George Wilson, who now coaches the Detroit Lions, played end. There were Joe Stydahar and Danny Fortmann and Bulldog Turner and a host of other giants among men in the line. And, above all, there was George Halas running the show. He could, somehow, inspire a tremendous *espirit de corps* in a pro football team and he did. The Bears wore their uniforms like a badge of honor and they still do, although it is a decade since a Bear team won a championship. George Halas and Sid Luckman and Joe Stydahar and George McAfee—they led the way into the new era of pro football—the age of the T.

The Quarterback Over Center

This is the first of the great T quarterbacks—Sid Luckman—over the first of the great T centers, Bulldog Turner. This combination—a great quarterback operating behind a great center—is still the keystone of the T attack, and very few have surpassed this first Bear duo.

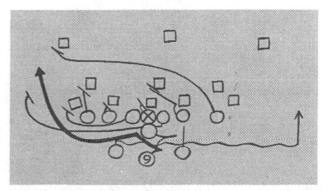

On the Bears' first play, Bill Osmanski scored. The play (above) was the first time a counter was used wherein the whole flow of play was to right, including Osmanski's first step. He then countered to left and went 60 yards for a touchdown, as George Wilson, the Bears' right end, took out Redskins' left half and safety with one block on sideline.

Evolution of the Helmet

THE FIRST HELMET was a good growth of long hair. Jim Thorpe and the players of the salad days of football wore whatever hirsute adornment they could muster to protect themselves from the buffeting of fate and the opposition's linemen. For a long time, a helmet was regarded as the mark of a sissy; in the early days of the pro game, a small concussion was a badge of success. Slowly, however, wise heads prevailed over hard ones, discretion became the better part of valor and the helmet became more and more common on both college and pro gridirons. Now, of course, a helmet is mandatory.

The early helmets were made of soft, thin leather and fitted snugly against the skull, so that they transmitted the shock of a blow almost undiluted. As the game progressed and the science of protection progressed with it, the helmets changed, too. They were changed from soft to hard leather, padded inside; that helped, but the driving shock of a knee on the side of the helmet could not be absorbed by the leather headgear.

Finally a gentleman named John T. Riddell developed the prototype of the modern helmet—a plastic shell suspended on webbing. The players, who, incidentally, never call a helmet anything but a hat, took to the Riddell hat at once. The Riddell suspension helmet could absorb far more impact than the old headgear; a web of straps fitting closely on the player's head kept the skull away from the skin of the helmet. The initial shock of a blow was distributed over the webbing so that there was no dangerous localized impact.

At its inception the Riddell hat was not perfect. Fred Naumetz, who was linebacker and captain of the Rams, split nine Riddell hats during one season of play. Naumetz was a violent, head-on tackler; despite the damaged hats, he survived uninjured. But the Riddell people, somewhat taken aback by the exuberance with which Naumetz destroyed their product, spent the off season redesigning their helmets. They have had no trouble since. All helmets use the suspension principal now, and it is safe to say that any football helmet in use today offers its wearer complete protection.

The Rams were responsible for another helmet change as well. Fred Gehrke, a Ram halfback who was a teammate of Naumetz, designed the first personalized team headgear. Gehrke, a commercial artist, designed a helmet with rams' horns curling over the ear holes. He and a crew of teammates spent the summer of 1948 drawing the design on the old Ram helmets, and on opening day the crowd reception was enthusiastic. But the battering of game action chipped the paint off and Gehrke and his assistants had to renew the paint job every week. The next year the symbol was baked into the plastic helmet, and the Ram hat started a trend which has become a part of football.

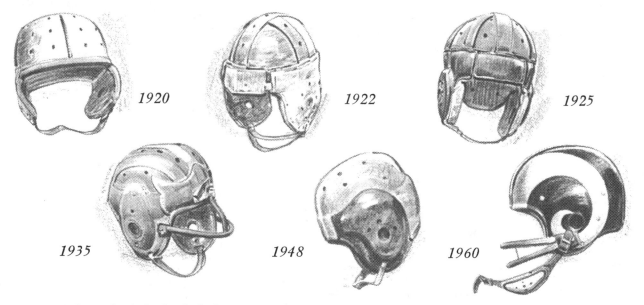

1920   *1922*   *1925*

1935   *1948*   *1960*

The colorful plastic helmet of today with its web suspensions and protective face bars is a far cry from the leather crown and earflaps of 1920. In 1922, the "reinforced" leather crossbands and forehead piece were added. From this came the "old helmet"—1925—that Grange wore, which remained more or less standard for 15 years. In the middle Thirties the first face guards appeared, and in the late Forties the molded leather hat was popular and is still used by some today.

The New League

W HEN WORLD WAR II ended, pro football had just begun to grow heartily. Because of this growth, a new football league—the All-America Conference — was started. It lasted four years, from 1946 through 1949, and then it died from malnutrition of the box office. During those four years, the most notable contribution the AAC made to pro football was the Cleveland Browns, a wonderfully conceived team, assembled, organized and operated by one of the real geniuses of pro football, a small, cold and brilliantly intelligent man named Paul Brown. The principal instrument of Brown's brilliance was a fine quarterback named Otto Graham, who can tell the story of the Browns—which is the story of the All-America Conference—better than anyone else:

"Paul approached me while I was in service in 1945 and offered me $250 a month for the rest of the war if I would sign with the Browns, which were still in the planning stage, so I did. I had been drafted by the Detroit Lions, but they didn't contact me. I was lucky to play with the Browns. All of us were new in pro football and I got the chance to play all the time right away. Paul at first wanted us to be a running team, but that didn't work. So we changed to passing and we developed a lot of the passing techniques that are successful today. Paul's concept of a pass was the perfect triangle." (See diagram below.) "Our receiver would go straight downfield maybe five or ten yards, then cut to the sideline, but instead of cutting at a right angle he would come back to the base of the triangle. That way he picked up a step or two on the defensive halfback and he was impossible to cover. We did it with ends or halfbacks and we really perfected it, although other teams used it too. And, of course, we used the trap with Motley to keep the defenses honest. I guess Marion Motley was the best fullback I ever saw. He could start like a rocket and run hard and was great on pass-protection blocking."

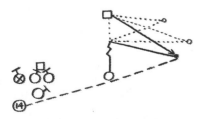

When the All-America Conference went out of business in 1949, the Browns survived. They survive still and they are, today, one of the great teams in pro football. Graham has retired, but Brown hasn't. He has won eleven titles in 14 years.

The Fullback

Marion Motley, above, was one of the great fullbacks of all time. He was a big man—around 240 lbs.—and he had tremendous speed. Not only all-out speed, but tremendous acceleration, which made him nearly impossible to stop on quick shots into the line or on the Motley trap (below). The trap was the perfect complement to Graham's passing—it forced the defenses to keep manpower in the middle and leave the deep passing areas insufficiently manned.

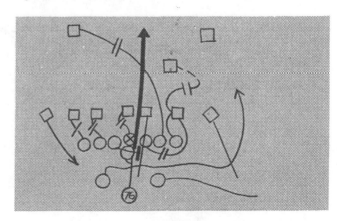

The Pros Move West

IN 1945, the Cleveland Rams won the world championship. They did it primarily on the wondrous performance of a rookie quarterback named Bob Waterfield (running his famous bootleg play above), who had played college football at UCLA. In 1946, Dan Reeves, the owner of the Rams, moved the team to Los Angeles; it was to prove the most intelligent move in the long history of pro football. Reeves did it in the face of strenuous opposition from the rest of the league; he had to walk out of the league meeting in New York and threaten to quit football before the other owners granted him permission to move.

In the next few years, the Rams struggled in competition with the Los Angeles Dons, but pro football was a perfect sport for the wild and woolly coast town. The fans poured out in increasing numbers to watch what had become the most explosive offense in the history of the game. Runners like Glenn Davis and Dick Hoerner and Vitamin Smith broke away for long gains or touchdowns; Waterfield himself was backstopped by a chubby, stubborn, slow-moving rookie quarterback from Oregon named Norman Van Brocklin. Van Brocklin could throw even better than Waterfield, and the two Ram quarterbacks had as targets the finest set of receivers in league history. Elroy Hirsch, Tom Fears, Bob Shaw—these were the targets, and in 1949, as the decade ended, they brought the Rams a division championship. The 1950 Ram team rewrote the league record book in passing offense and, more important, began to make money. Reeves, who had fought the strength of the old established owners in moving, was justified. The All-America Conference died and with it went the Ram opposition in Los Angeles, the Dons. Also, the San Francisco 49ers, a team which had played in the AAC, joined the NFL, setting up the most exciting, lucrative series in the league. Now pro football draws crowds of over 100,000 to the Los Angeles Coliseum.

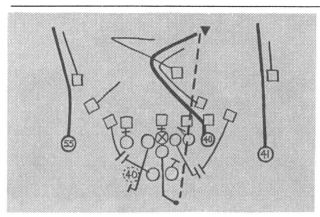

The three ends:

With two great quarterbacks and a trio of incomparable passcatchers, the Rams invented a new offense: three primary receivers. At first two backs and an end were used and later three ends. They moved a halfback, Elroy (Crazylegs) Hirsch (40), into the line as right end with Tom Fears (55) on the left side and halfback Glenn Davis (41) out as a flanker a yard back of the line (later the third end played this spot). In 1950 these three caught 168 passes. They routed the Colts 70-27 and in their 65-24 win over the Lions scored 41 points in the third quarter. Until the defense caught up, this wonderful offense seemed unstoppable.

The Rule of the Rough Eagle

OR SOME REASON or other, pro football teams develop a sort of corporate personality. Over the years, regardless of personnel, a team will be a personality in itself. Maybe the toughest personality in the league, during the 1940s, was the Philadelphia Eagles. Their coach was a tough man named Greasy Neale, an ex-major-league baseball player and, too, an ex-pro-football player from the days of the Canton Bulldogs and the Frankford Yellowjackets. Greasy was—and is—an uncomplicated man. He taught an uncomplicated offense based on the theory that the best way to advance a football is to knock down every one in the way. The story that Greasy once outlined his whole offensive repertoire on the back of a brown paper sack is very likely apocryphal—but it catches the spirit of Neale and of his team.

The Eagles, in their heyday, had only a few plays. Steve Van Buren, a tremendously powerful and elusive runner (below), would start wide around the end, then cut back quickly, plow the linebacker under and run crunchingly over a couple of defensive halfbacks. (Diagram at right.) Or Tommy Thompson, a one-eyed quarterback who threw better than most men with two eyes, would toss a short screen pass to Pete Pihos. Pihos had been a fullback at Indiana; once he caught the screen, he proceeded along an undeviating line through and over the opposition. It wasn't fancy, but it worked. The Eagles won a divisional title in 1947 and world championships in 1948 and 1949 before they grew, collectively, too old and tired. When they were young and lusty, they were a sight to behold. Once the Rams, just reaching manhood in Los Angeles, came to Philadelphia riding a six-game winning streak, with a tip-off on Thompson. They knew he would hand off to the right if his right foot was back, to the left if his left was, and drop back to pass if his feet were even when he took the snap from center. The Eagles beat the Rams by four touchdowns simply by running over them—the mark of the Eagles.

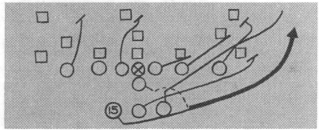

The 1948 Championship
The 1948 world championship was played in a snowstorm in Philadelphia, and the Eagles won, 7-0, over the Cardinals. Van Buren, running as powerfully as ever in the snow, scored the only touchdown.

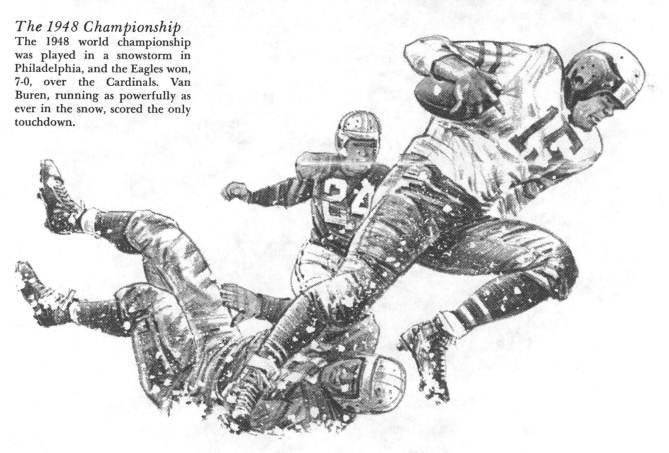

Part Two

THE GREAT DECADE

1950-1960

AS THE FIFTIES BEGAN, two things happened to make professional football's slow, steady growth suddenly explode. The All-America Conference, formed in 1946 in the immediate post-war sports boom, died of malnutrition of the box office, leaving the field to the older, stronger National Football League. Three teams from the AAC joined the NFL—the Cleveland Browns, the San Francisco 49ers and the Baltimore Colts. Television, spreading its coaxial cables across the face of the United States like a giant octopus, became a tremendous factor in the promotion of sports. And, of the major sports, only professional football made wise use of the muscle of the new giant of entertainment. Major-league baseball, greedily gobbling the TV dollars, squeezed minor-league baseball dry. The small fight clubs which nurture young boxers went out of business in the face of competition from TV boxing shows. But the NFL, under the wise guidance of Commissioner Bert Bell, used TV as a showcase for its great football teams. No vised its road games back to the home-town fans. The televised road games whetted the interest of team televised its home games, and every team tele-the fans, and the curve of attendance started a sharp rise.

The pro game was attuned to the temper of the times, too. This was the violent generation, fresh from the wars. Baseball was too slow and too quiet; it was the game of an earlier America, not of the jet age. College football turned to the Split-T, surely one of the dullest attacks to watch in the whole history of football. The philosophy of the Split-T was contained in the phrase "three yards and a cloud of dust." This was the battle strategy of World War I, the infantry slogging slowly ahead.

The pros, to continue the battle analogy, used the tactical approach of World War II: the swift strike of a tank battalion in lighting-fast sweeps by big, quick fullbacks, the devastating effect of an air strike in the superb passing of wonderfully capable quarterbacks throwing to the finest ends and half-backs in the game.

The difference in pro and college football was painfully apparent. College games were televised on Saturday afternoon, pro games on Sunday. And, as the watching audience grew, the difference in spectator appeal was spelled out at the ticket windows. The Los Angeles Rams, long the third team in Los Angeles, behind UCLA and USC, edged up to even and then moved well ahead of the two college teams in total attendance. In Detroit, several thousand people stood in line through the bitter cold of a December night waiting for the ticket windows to open so they could buy tickets to a championship game. The crowd surging around a ticket booth at San Francisco's Kezar Stadium up-rooted the booth and it came down on a hopeful fan's foot. No one helped him until the few general admission tickets on sale were all gone.

The heroes of the fifties, like the game itself, seemed larger than life-size. The incomparable Otto Graham executed the strategies of Cleveland Coach Paul Brown with delicate precision. (Bob Riger's stunning portrait of this potent combine is at left.) Bob Waterfield and Norm Van Brocklin of the Rams mounted the most explosive offensive in the history of football in Los Angeles, throwing to pass receivers like Elroy Hirsch, Tom Fears and Glenn Davis. The excitement, the crowds, the fanaticism grew and is still growing. The prospects for the next ten years are overwhelming.

The Devotion

Sam Huff (above) is a linebacker for the New York Giants. Time was when he labored in comparative obscurity, performing his heroics practically unnoticed by the average football fan. But, with the burgeoning growth of pro football, the knowledgeable fan has begun to give the stars of the defense their due. Huff, trotting onto the field to a fanfare from the Giant band, elicits a swelling roar of ap-

to a Game

proval from Yankee Stadium Giant fans. At left, the shapely baton twirlers for the Los Angeles Rams are performing before a sizable group of Ram fans who have made the 400-mile trek from Los Angeles to San Francisco for a game with the 49ers. In Baltimore's Memorial Stadium (right) the fans come early to hang out the home-made signs indicative of their devotion to the Colts. All over the

league, this truly fanatic loyalty to the home team is apparent. The explosion of interest in professional football crosses social, economic and intellectual lines. The top executives of America's motor industry are season-ticket holders in Detroit, along with their employees. And a good percentage of any pro-football crowd is made up of women. The kids, of course, come by the thousands.

The TV Bonanza

Seldom have a sport and a medium for its presentation meshed so neatly as pro football and television. Football is, to coin a word, telegenic. Pro football is especially telegenic. And the owners of the professional football teams, in the early fifties, came fresh from a hideously costly war with the All America Conference. They welcomed TV money, but they knew, first hand, the danger of overexposure. When each major city had two — and sometimes three — pro football teams with games for thirteen or fourteen consecutive Sundays, the sport suffered. So the pro owners handled TV gingerly and well. And the TV people did their job nobly, too. Professional football is presented crisply and accurately on TV. The announcers and the color men, as often as not, are ex-players like Elroy Hirsch or John Lujack or Tom Harmon, and they can point up and convey the violent charm of the game perfectly. The picture to the right probably made you vaguely uneasy when you looked at it; it's from the pre-TV era, and you find it unfamiliar because both teams are wearing dark jerseys. Since 1956, when CBS began a full-scale program of regional televising of pro games, it has been a rule of the NFL that the visiting team wear white jerseys and the home team dark. The picture was made in 1953 and it shows the Philadelphia Eagles' Bobby Thomason passing against the New York Giants. The tackle climbing over the stacked humanity in front of Thomason is an all-time all-pro —the Giants' Arnie Weinmeister. It's a great picture and it shows that the essential conflict which makes pro football popular is unchanged. But Thomason and Weinmeister, great as they were, were known only to a comparatively few fans. TV makes today's superstars—the Giffords and Huffs, Unitases and Berrys—familiar to a nation.

The Quarterback

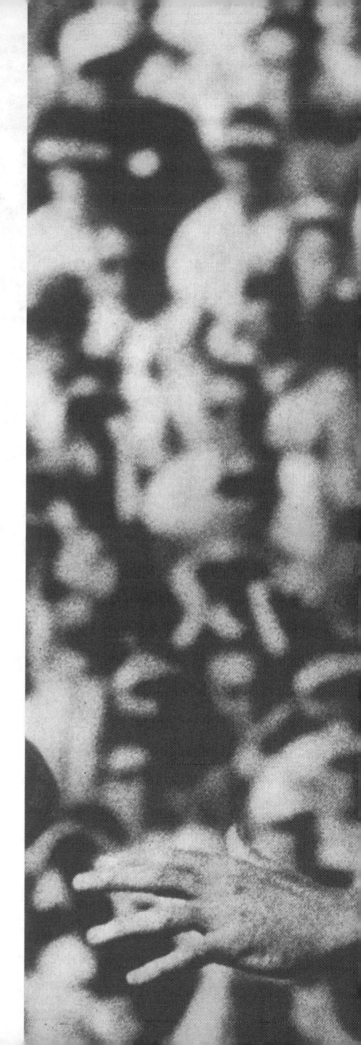

Professional football is a game for specialists. The men who play it can do one thing, or a combination of a few things, superlatively well. In this gallery of stars, only one does a number of things very, very well. He is the loneliest man in football—the quarterback. Ideally, he passes with the instinctive accuracy of a Kentucky rifleman, fakes as coolly as the operator of a carnival shell game and runs as thoughtfully as a fox before the hounds. He must know all the complexities of a modern pro offense faultlessly and he must be able to command this wide range of information instantly, in the 25 seconds between offensive plays. Not all quarterbacks, of course, can do all of this. Billy Wade, the Ram quarterback on this spread, comes close but lacks the X ingredient—leadership. Bobby Layne and Charlie Conerly, on the next two pages, are incomparable leaders, but Layne is not a great faker and Conerly is not a great passer. Norman Van Brocklin, on the page following, passes magnificently and fakes well, but Dutch is a stubborn man who sometimes overlooks the subtleties of tactics to prove an unprovable point. Not until you get to the last quarterback shown in this gallery (pages 38–39) do you find the one who has—so far—combined all the qualities of greatness. John Unitas throws with unbelievable accuracy; he fakes with the insouciant assurance of a riverboat gambler; he runs resourcefully and well, and he has the ineffable quality of leadership which is the *sine qua non* of great quarterbacks. Now, early in his career, he seems to be the perfect quarterback; it remains to be seen whether the erosion of time and tackling wears away that promise. Unitas has evolved out of Sid Luckman and Bob Waterfield and Bobby Layne and Otto Graham and Charlie Conerly and Norman Van Brocklin—or so it seems.

Deception

In football, as in battle, the surest way to success is to outnumber the enemy at the point of attack. Since there are eleven men on each side of the scrimmage line, the only way to get there "fustest with the mostest" is by deception. The quarterback must make the defense overload away from the place where the play will strike; in these pictures Milt Plum of the Browns and Eddie LeBaron of the Washington Redskins are doing just that. At top, Plum is extending his empty hand to fullback Jim Brown, cutting into the middle of the line. After Brown has drawn the attention of the defending lineman, Plum will hand off to the halfback going wide. The ball, meanwhile, is tucked out of sight in Plum's belly. Below, LeBaron stretches wide to give the ball to Olszewski (0)—or does he? Look again. Eddie has already given the ball to halfback Watson (41) going left.

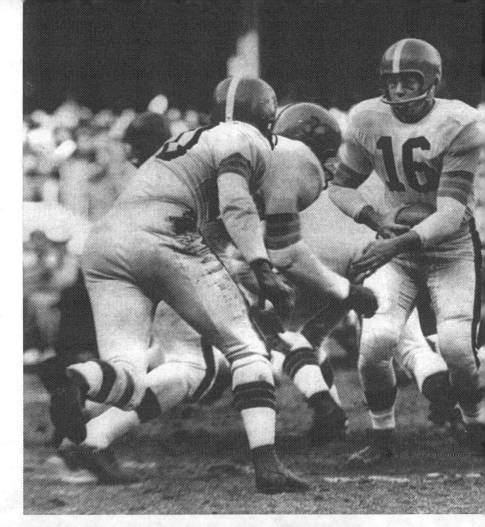

Pressure

Pressure is the climate of the quarterback's life. How well he lives with it and how he reacts to it determine how good he is. Here San Francisco's Y. A. Tittle is the victim of the crushing weight of pressure in a game with the Baltimore Colts in Baltimore. Top left, Tittle unloads a gasp ahead of being hit by Colt linebacker Don Shinnick. Bottom left, the gap narrows and Tittle is pinched between airborne Colts Dick Szysmanski and Ordell Braase. Top right, Pellington (36), Joyce (83) and Marchetti (89) apply irresistible pressure. Bottom right, Tittle, injured by the stunning three-way tackle, crouches tentatively on a crippled leg; Colt tackle Art Donovan (70) watches with the faint, cold smile of a real old pro.

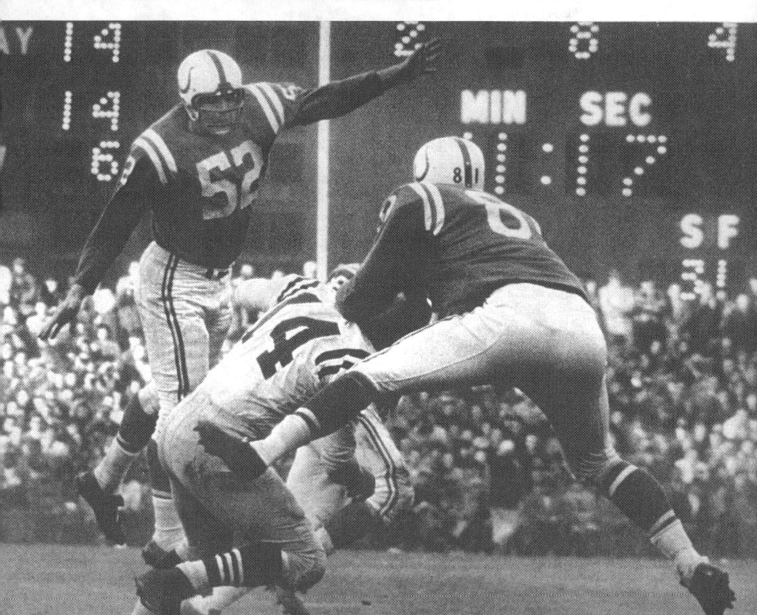

1

Here is Unitas: brilliant, devastating, striking in the wink of an eye. The threat of this almost unstoppable pass sets up the familiar fake which makes the play on page 168 so effective.

2

Svare (84), the Giant (right side) linebacker, must get out very fast to cover. Unitas has spun and cocked his arm ready to throw in the fraction of a second Ameche needs for one stride.

3

The ball is away now (just ahead of Unitas' helmet), and Svare, seeing it coming right at him, blinks. Raymond Berry (82), the receiver, has come into the picture (left), Lynch (22) covering.

4

Svare turns, throws up his hands instinctively to try to deflect the ball (above numeral 8) which goes by his ear like a bullet. Berry is ready for the catch.

5

Berry is the focus of a triangle including Unitas and Svare. Lynch is coming up desperately from the rear and Jim Patton (20) is hurrying over from his deep safety spot to lend aid.

6

The ball is home, clutched to Berry's stomach, and the pass is complete despite the efforts of three Giant defenders to stop it. Berry is already beginning to turn down field for more yards.

7

Berry's quick spin makes Patton overrun the tackle and Svare, too, misjudges his route. Lynch makes the tackle as Berry digs hard for the yards he needs to get the Colts a first down.

8

Berry, running heavily with Lynch's weight bearing down on him, picked up five yards after the catch. Elapsed time, from pass to tackle, was, amazingly, only eight tenths of a second.

The Halfback

The modern pro halfback is bigger and stronger than the fullback of thirty years ago — and much faster. The very best ones, such as the Giants' Frank Gifford (opposite) or Baltimore's Lennie Moore (next page), represent the most versatile weapon for attack in the arsenal of football. They run with power and deception and with a sixth sense which allows them to plot a safe course through the scattered tacklers in a broken field. They catch passes as sure-handedly as an end. When the occasion demands, they block on a massive linebacker or defensive end with ferocity and, usually, with effect. Gifford, shown here running one of the most difficult plays in football to contain, adds accurate passing to his other talents. On this option, Gifford swings wide, behind a blocker like big Rosey Brown (79), and then throws, if a receiver has worked into the clear, or runs with the ball if the defenders have dropped away from him to cover against the pass. Nearly all pro halfbacks combine running and pass-catching talents; only Gifford and two or three others can throw as well. Most of the halfbacks are fine actors, too. They slash into the line with as much fire and determination on a fake handoff, without the ball, as they do when they are actually carrying it. In the delicate timing of a pro play, the halfback's convincing feint is designed to create a fleeting, immobilizing doubt in a key defender, giving a blocker time to reach and erase him.

Most pro teams carry one or two halfbacks who specialize almost entirely in carrying the ball. They are not especially good blockers or receivers and often they are not big enough to accept the savage punishment full-time service entails. They are spot players like Los Angeles' Jon Arnett or Detroit's Hopalong Cassady, and they provide, with their heart-stopping long runs, some of the finest moments in the game.

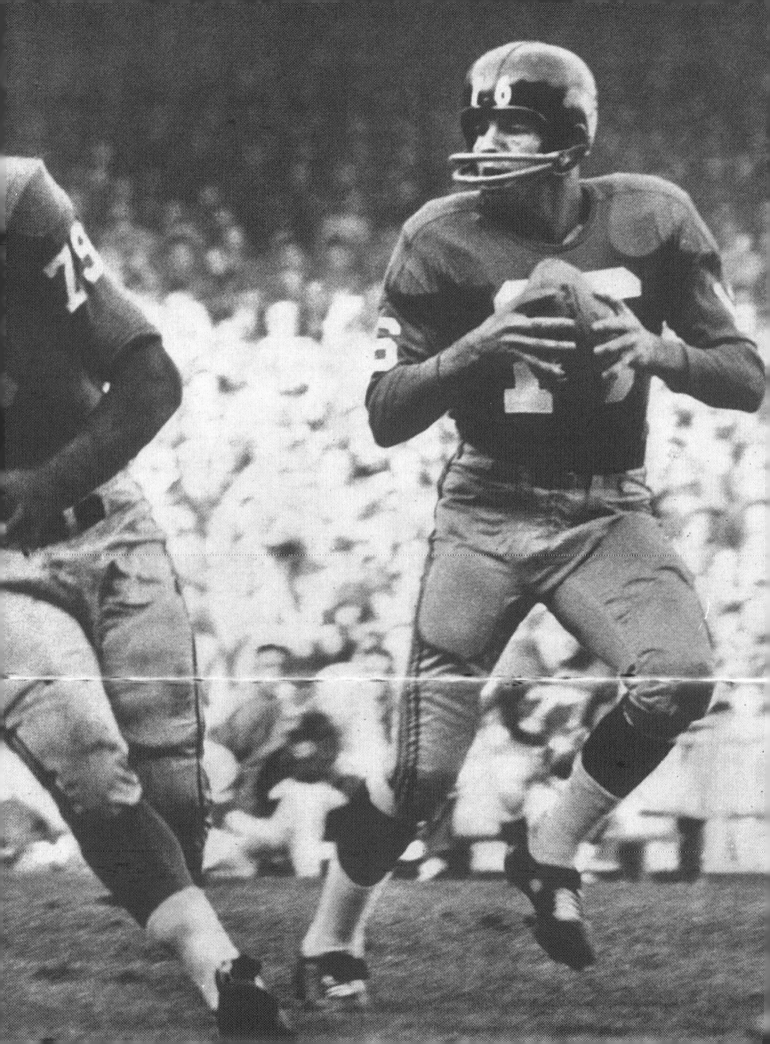

These are two of the wonderful waterbugs of pro football—the small, mouse-quick halfbacks who live dangerously among the behemoths of the business. When an Arnett (left) or a Cassady (above) finds the small running room he needs to start the intricate, weaving pattern of a great run, he's all little men everywhere.

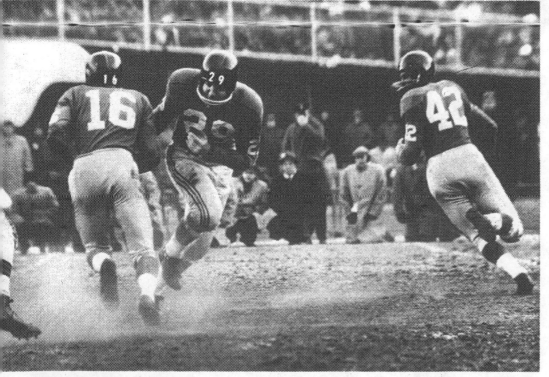

Working Together

The Giants' handsome halfback tandem of Alex Webster (far left) and Frank Gifford is a perfect combination of speed, power and versatility. Years of working together have made them almost intuitive in their knowledge of each other's reactions; at the left, they collaborate on a delicately timed reverse from Webster to Gifford which ended in a touchdown pass to Conerly (42).

49

The Fullback

In the firepower of a football team, the fullback represents the heavy-weapons section. He must have the size—and most of them do—to batter headlong into the mass of a pro defensive line and move it. But he must have the speed to wheel outside end, too, and most of them can. A fullback of the stature of Ollie Matson (right and page 58) is worth a team of lesser players, and that's what the Rams gave the Cardinals for Matson. Matson is a fleet, powerful and deceptive runner who is equally adept at taking a quick pitchout to go outside or bursting through the middle. Like Cleveland's incomparable Jim Brown, who may prove to be the greatest fullback of all time, Matson is a constant threat to go all the way; fullbacks like the Bears' Rick Casares (below) or Alan Ameche of Baltimore start with the instant acceleration of a fighting bull and hit with shattering impact but are not, like Brown and Matson, capable of converting a five-yard gain into fifty by outrunning the defensive backs. Much of the success of the better air attacks in the league depends on the blocking ability of the fullbacks, who must be able to meet and delay the charge of a giant lineman until the quarterback makes his throw.

Here is Alan (the Horse) Ameche of the Baltimore Colts doing superbly well what is the first requirement of every fullback. Ameche, near the goal line, has taken a handoff from Johnny Unitas. Already, in three steps, he is moving at top speed, the ball firmly clutched in both arms and his 240 pounds slanting low and hard into the ruck of the scrimmage. The Colt blocking is nearly perfect. Defend-

er number 63, spinning off a block, may get around in time to get an arm on Ameche, but no good fullback is stopped by an arm tackle. By the time Ameche clears this gaping hole, the defensive half-backs will have the thankless task of trying to stop him, but his perfect form—low, legs wide for balance, knees high—will carry him another five yards after the tackle — enough for the first down.

1

Jim Brown, football's finest full-back, shows the almost incredible speed which animates his 228 pounds. On Cleveland's first play from scrimmage against the Giants, Brown's off.

2

He popped through a quick hole off guard and was suddenly into the secondary, already moving at near top speed. Converging on him are Crowe (41), Patton (20) and Svare (84), all fast.

3

Svare gets a hand on Brown, who shrugs it off easily. Patton and Crowe appear to have him hemmed in, however. Their angle of pursuit is good, and both of them are capable, sure tacklers.

4

Now Brown has accelerated again and, amazingly, run out of the reach of Crowe and Patton, who is reaching hopelessly and desperately. Brown went 65 yards on this touchdown play.

Brown, on a kickoff return, is cutting sharply, his cleats kicking up a spurt of dust, his body beautifully balanced, the toughest man in the league to tackle. On the next page, he's well on his way, outrunning his blockers, leaving a trail of would-be tacklers sprawled in his wake.

The Kicker

Crouched intently, the ball held with delicate precision so that the laces are to the front, Charlie Conerly of the Giants awaits a place-kick. "I'm just a third of a successful place-kick," says Cleveland's Lou Groza, the greatest kicker of all. "Most people forget the holder and the guy who centers the ball. They're as important as I am." Groza, shown on the next page just before a kick, has exaggerated a little; the kicker is still the most important man in a field goal or extra-point try. For the pros, place-kicking is a precise art; the good kickers are amazingly accurate from as far out as 50 yards and nearly infallible inside the 30-yard line. The perfect timing of the double pendulum action of the right leg produces this accuracy. On the next page, the camera has caught Groza in the crucial moment of the kick as the left foot is planted.

The Automatic Pointmakers

The extra point in professional football has, for years, been almost conceded. The place-kickers, through long hours of unrelenting practice, have become, in effect, single-digit adding machines who tack on their small increment almost unnoticed by the crowd. They perform their chore in an odd never-never land of the game; the clock does not run during an extra-point try, so that a specialist who does nothing but kick extra points might out-score the best halfback in the league in a season and not record a single minute of playing time. Their moments of glory come on the long game-winning field goals; few moments in football have been more dramatic than the 49-yarder Pat Summerall lofted through a snow storm in the closing seconds to give the Giants a victory over Cleveland in 1958 and put them into the championship playoff. Summerall (shown at right kicking an extra point) bids fair to take over as the game's best place-kicker when Cleveland's great Lou Groza hangs up his cleats. Summerall is a specialist who does little else for the Giants; Groza is a very good offensive tackle as well. Doak Walker (left, below), the tiny halfback who won immortality with the Lions, counted place-kicking as only one of many accomplishments. George Blanda (right, below) came to the Chicago Bears as a quarterback, but he is remembered as one of the most consistent of all the adding machines (247 extra points in 250 tries). One thing they all had: the protection of a perfectly co-ordinated blocking team, as shown next page.

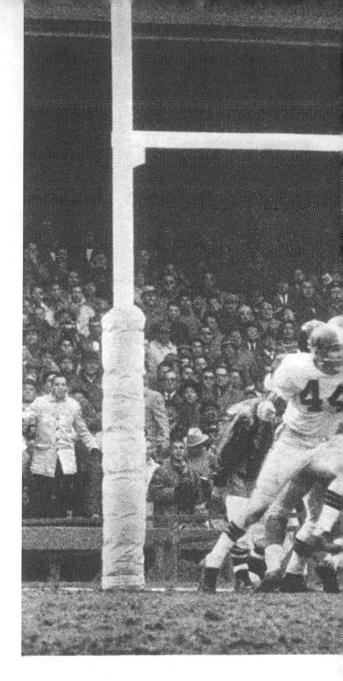

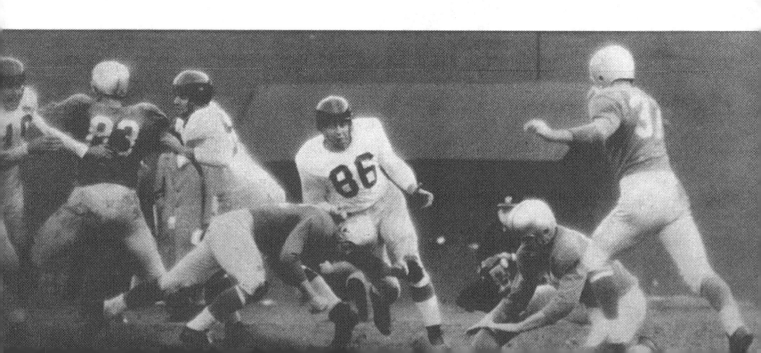

A good punter is absolutely essential but rare; punting is a difficult and demanding art. Here's the technique perfectly shown as if by one kicker but actually by three of the best: the kicker balanced (Don Chandler); the ball dropped precisely flat and level (Tommy Davis); and the powerful follow-through (Dave Sherer).

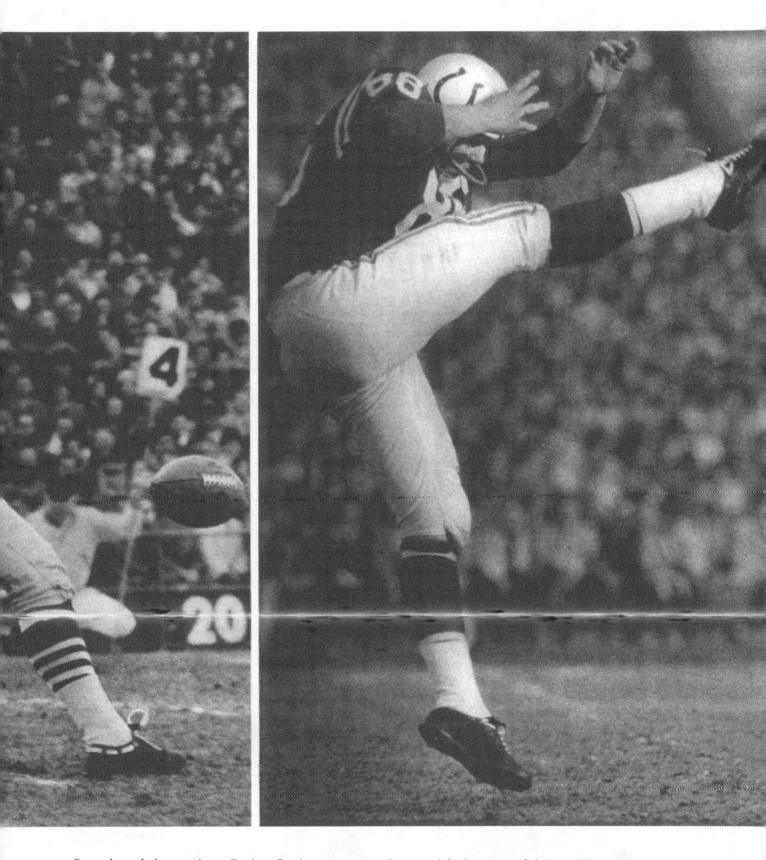

Properly used, the punt is an effective offensive weapon as well as one of the keys to good defense. The sure knowledge that your punter can boom the ball 50 yards or more downfield allows the quarterback to play a more daring game; conversely, if these booming punts keep a team deep in its own territory, it can't gamble.

The Pass-Catchers

In football, as in war, this is the era of the guided missile. But half of the air attack in football depends on the pass-catcher. Says Red Hickey, a former end and now coach of the San Francisco 49ers: "The first thing an end must have is a willing disregard of the consequences." Baltimore's wonderful trio of receivers all have that, plus marvelous ability to fake into the clear, and wonderfully delicate, sensitive hands. Below, Raymond Berry, the most intellectual and knowledgeable end who ever played the game, looks like a matador as he leans gracefully over the sideline to catch a pass, his feet carefully planted inbounds. His whole body is drawn to the ball and he is completely concentrated on it. This concentration and the strong, reaching hands are the mark of a great receiver. All the fine ones, including the great Del Shofner of the Rams (next page), look oddly alike at the moment the ball reaches them, their whole being drawn into their hands. Pass-catching is a complicated, demanding trade. It encompasses trickery, good acting on fakes, an encyclopedic knowledge of the defensive halfbacks in the league, plus, of course, "disregard of the consequences."

Here the Colts' Jim Mutscheller comes in for a two-point landing after having taken a pass under considerable duress. In the split second of falling, Mutscheller has, like all good ends, tucked the ball away.

Below, in one of the graceful moments which make pro football an aesthetic pleasure as well as an exciting sport to watch, Baltimore's Lennie Moore leaps high and far to cradle the ball gently on his finger tips. The ball was thrown so accurately that Moore, at top speed, could catch it almost in stride.

The ball is in the air and the passer and the receiver are committed, irretrievably. In the next split second the ball finds its target, the pass-catcher whirls and looks for the defense. Kyle Rote of the Giants (above), one eye gleaming savagely, tucks the ball away as he begins to take violent evasive action.

The Ballet of
the Secondary

Next to a great quarterback, the most precious discovery for a pro talent scout is a great defensive halfback. For a defensive halfback must have all the speed of the fleetest runner, the hands of a superb end, the courage of a lion, the reactions of a hunting cat and the intuition of a woman. Given all that, no one defensive back can cover a good receiver man on man consistently. The reason is simple: the receiver knows where he is going; the defender must react after the move has been made. He must be ready in an instant to come up fast and meet a hard-running fullback head on (below), or he must drop back even faster to leap high in the air and bat away a pass (right). Defensive backs are most effective when they work together as a unit over a period of years, so that their knowledge of each other's reactions becomes second nature. Yale Larry (28), on page 76, was part of a Detroit unit including Jack Christiansen, which may have been the best.

The glory is great and the disgrace is absolute in the life of a defensive back; he may, like the poetic Detroit defender (left), glide gracefully into the air for a key interception to stop the enemy attack; or, like the lonely, desperate back above, he may misjudge the pass, then miss the tackle and lose a game.

The Legendary Lineman

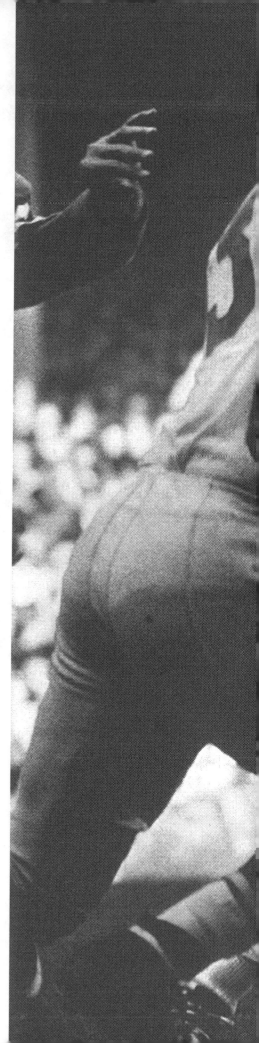

Someone has described the yard of space which separates the offensive from the defensive line in pro football as "no man's land." It's an apt description; football games are won or lost by control of this narrow strip of ground. The battle for it is a violent one. It is fought by the biggest, strongest athletes in all of the sports world, and the impact of these giants a split second after the snap of the ball is clearly audible in fieldside seats. Aside from the sound of leather on leather, plastic on plastic as helmets and pads crack together, there's the noise of curses, shouts, grunts and groans—always a surprise to a rookie in his first pro football game. The heroes of this bitter infighting were once nameless men who labored mightily almost unnoticed by the spectators, who watched the more spectacular antics of the ball carriers. Now, by virtue of the increasing expertise of pro crowds and by virtue, too, of the importance of defense, the behemoths who man the front-line trenches are nearly as well known as a Gifford or a Tittle or a Layne. Men like Big Daddy Lipscomb, the 290-pound Baltimore tackle, or Andy Robustelli, the 250-pound Giant end, draw clusters of small boys when they leave the dressing room after a game, just like the backs. (Lipscomb is very much aware of his responsibility to his young fans. Asked once why he picks up a ball carrier after tackling him, Big Daddy said, "It's because I don't want the kids to think Big Daddy is a cruel man.") Sometimes it's a desperate, almost impossible job, as you can see if you study the faces of the eleven lonely men awaiting the attack with the ball on their one-inch line (pages 88, 89). Now there's no more ground to give and the odds are insuperable, the touchdown certain. But sometimes they hold and the roar of the crowd is shattering after the still moment of waiting.

The big men move with power and precision and surprising agility. Here a mighty guard and a tackle have pulled out to sweep a path for the San Francisco ball carrier on an end run.

The ball has just been handed off and to the right and in the background you can see the debris left by the primary blocks in the line, but the blockers and the runner are concentrating on the road ahead.

Run or Pass

The blocking job for a lineman varies considerably, depending on whether the play is a pass or a run. On a run, the blocker's job is to knock a defender down; on a pass, he keeps his feet and stays between the incoming lineman and the passer. To the left, the blocker in the background has made the mistake of falling to the ground so that the tackler is jumping over him; the other blocker has left the ground, may be played off by the tackler. Below, the Colt line is giving Unitas perfect protection, each man blocking out his defender perfectly.

The Faces of the Tiger

The linemen meet face to face across the narrow strip of the scrimmage line. The faces are always intent, concentrated. The eyes move back and forth, slyly seeking the tip-off, the small telltale motion or attitude which will indicate where the play is going, or how the defense will react. Behind the helmet bars the big men stare at one another, coldly impassive, until the snap of the ball, when the distortions of anger, pain, disgust, joy and, sometimes, fear twist the faces. All the linemen wear the bars across the front of the helmet for protection now; not too long ago, the bars were rare. The mark of a good lineman then was a toothless smile; that meant that the player kept his head up and inevitably a knee or an elbow or a foot knocked out his front teeth. It's as rough, but safer, now.

All the violence and impact of pro football lives in this remarkable photograph. The runner is a big man but he is dwarfed by bigger men. The first tackler to reach him (42) has his left hand under the ball, may tug it loose in one of the first rules of pro tackling—go for the ball. Coming up fast are five more tacklers who will smash into the runner in the next split second. Gang tackling, seen from the stands, seems unnecessarily brutal; actually, a team that doesn't gang tackle sees the agile, twisting

runners of the National Football League pull away
from single tacklers time and again to go for long
gains or for touchdowns. The runners accept this
as one of the occupational hazards of their trade
and they survive the impact very well.

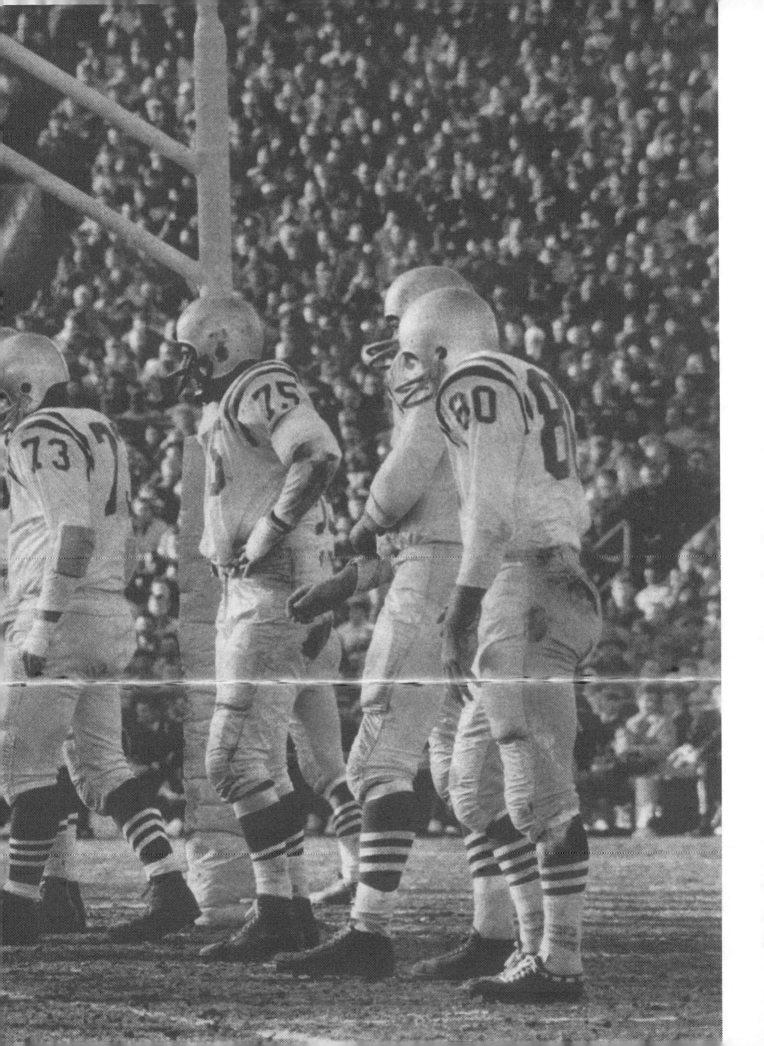

The Hand-to-Hand
Battle in the Line

Under the rules of football, only the defensive lineman is allowed the use of his hands in line play. Under the more elemental law of survival, the fight in the line is a hand-to-hand struggle, and the hands involved in it are usually about the size of a Virginia ham. The bandages you see on the massive paws at the right are not necessarily there to protect an old injury, or even to prevent a new one. Often they are used for the same reason a boxer uses bandages under his gloves—to provide a more compact, tightly knit striking device. There was a time when some pro linemen wore uncovered plaster casts on their hands and wrists, but this was too lethal a weapon; now a cast must be adequately padded. These hands are just as powerful as they look, too; Ed Neal, the old middle guard for the Green Bay Packers, used to open beer bottles by flipping the top off with his thumbnail. When he had emptied the bottle, usually in one gargantuan gulp, he would sometimes dispose of it by breaking it over an iron-hard forearm. He was not unique.

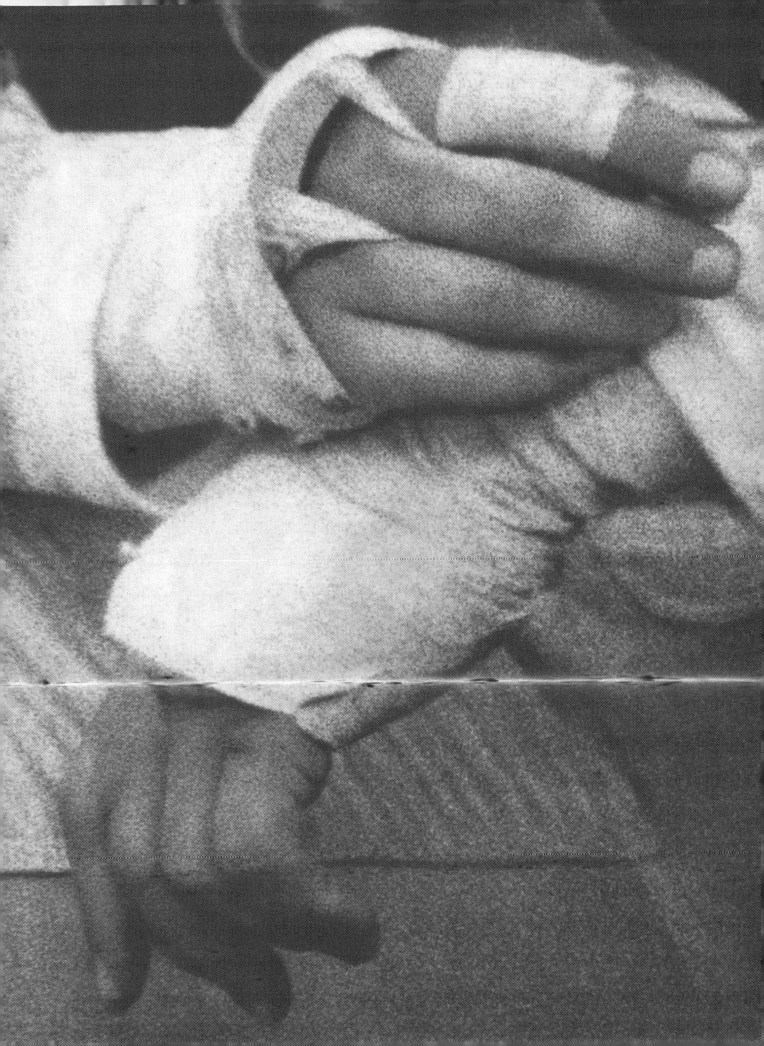

Behind the trustful quarterback (42), the players joust. On the result of these individual duels depends the success of the play and the good health of the quarterback. This epic picture picks out three battles: 89 and 77, far left, trying to

strangle one another; 62 and 55 rooster fighting; and the giant 76 holding off his foe with a massive arm as he blinds him by tipping his helmet down with one finger and gains a precious second to "read" how the play will go.

The big men meet in elemental, violent conflict and no one sees them. These dramatic pictures show the brute force of the linemen in action: the shocking impact of a block, the awesome size of a defensive tackle. The trench warfare of the line is tough and bitter and, always, man against man.

The Linebacker

The linebackers are the shock troops of the defense; they are thrown into the melee of the line to help stem a ground attack, they are sent wide to cover the flanks, and, on occasion, they drop back into the secondary line of defense to fend off an air strike. Theirs is probably the most demanding single assignment in football; on a typical play, a corner backer may be required first to hold up the offensive end, second, cover against a running play, then, third, drop back into the short-pass area to cover a receiver. These are the tough, hard-bitten pros — men like Sam Huff and Walt Michaels and Bill George, who glory in the bruising body contact of their trade. They must be smart and intuitive. The steady stare of the linebacker peering across at the quarterback on the opposite side reflects his concentration. He's going over a mental check list while the signals are called: down, position on the field, score, known habits of this quarterback, personnel in the game. If he interprets his data correctly, he'll have a half-step start; if not, he may cost his team a first down. Below, like kids on a street corner looking for a fight, the defenders wait for action.

Red Dog

Some teams call it "red dog," some call it "blitz," but the quarterbacks call it murder. Whatever it's called, it means that one or two, sometimes all three, of the linebackers fire through the line with the linemen, bent on wreaking mayhem on the passer before he can unload. "Red dog" is usually called in an obvious passing situation—say, third and long yardage for a first down. It's dangerous for the defense, too; if a wily quarterback calls a trap or a screen pass, he'll catch the defense with its fence down for a long gain. Below, red-dogging Sam Huff of the Giants has run head on into a jarring block. The force of the impact and of Huff's effort to slip the block and make the tackle on the runner shows in the corded muscles of his neck, the distorted grimace on his face. At the right, Huff is preparing to blast into Pittsburgh's Bobby Layne, who has cocked his arm but who may not get the pass away before Huff's 230 pounds batter him to the ground. This is a classic example of the red dog; the rushing defensive line, augmented by the linebackers, has slipped one man through the blocking screen by sheer weight of numbers—seven rushers against six blockers. On the next page, you can almost feel the shock as Huff slams into the ball carrier, his arms wrapped in a bear hug, legs wide spread, the runner beginning to topple and the play crushed. Because theirs is possibly the most spectacular of the defensive positions, linebackers often become the darlings of the knowledgeable fans. When Huff is introduced at Yankee Stadium, the buffs who buy standing-room tickets chant, happily, "Huff, Huff, Huff."

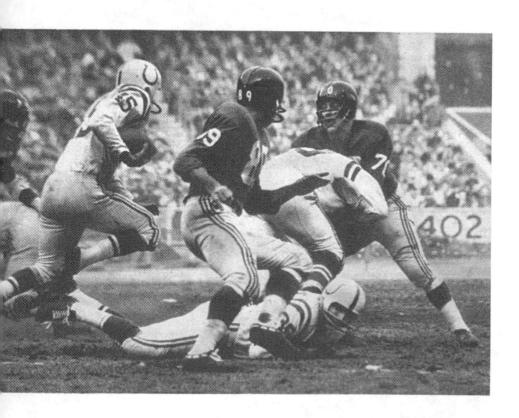

Speed
and Pursuit

The blistering speed at which pro football is played is shown clearly in these extraordinary photographs. The focus of attention — runner, blocker or tackler—is sharp and clear, and the blurred figures of the pursuers translate the rapidity of the action. At right, a runner peers anxiously ahead as the tacklers close in and a speeding blocker tries to give him help. Below, on a kickoff return, a small halfback heads into the valley of destruction, slanting gracefully away from a potential tackler, never losing speed. Below, right, a blocker (77), his eyes in perfect focus, looks calculatingly at the object of his attention (81), while the play spins away to his left. These pictures give you the feel of the pursuit in the game that you miss from far back in the stands, where the very distance disguises the violence and the swiftness of the action. Only from the sidelines, where the men and the mass and the speed are in proper proportion, can you appreciate the amazing speed. Or through these pictures.

One Man
to Beat

The success of a play, a game or a season comes down to the individual effort of one player very often. To no one is this more apparent than the safety man, whose mistakes cost touchdowns, not yards. Like the Green Bay halfback (47 at left), he is always alone. Above, the Giants' Jim Patton, possibly the finest safety in the game, slides off Chicago's Harlan Hill. Hill scored on a 79-yard pass from Bill McColl to give the Bears a 17-17 tie and the Western Division championship in 1956. Below, Patton's one-finger tackle saves a touchdown which would have cost the Giants the Eastern crown in 1958. It was the final game of the season; Patton's save gave it to New York 13-10.

The Bench

The old pro in his last season comes to it gratefully and sits head down, gasping for air. The young one stands along the sideline or fidgets restlessly, anxious to get back to the game. The mood of the bench swings with the tide of play: happy, glum, tense, angry, relaxed. It's the worst place in the park to watch a game—at ground level in midfield. The coach and his assistants stand or squat and stare intently at the field, but then retire to the substitute quarterback manning the phone. The coach high in the press box relays the information to the bench; height and distance resolve the confusion into a recognizable pattern. "It's a little world," one player said. "You don't hear the crowd. You watch and you don't see much. Sometimes you get up and walk to relieve the tension. You don't talk much. Maybe, sometimes, when a game is won. You may talk and laugh then. Or maybe you're too tired by then." When a game is lost, or well on the way to being lost, the bench is quiet and the strong faces grow still and watchful. The only happiness for the proud ones is victory.

A veteran halfback explains a mistake and an old tackle sits wordlessly, waiting for his defensive unit to return to action. The wide backs of the Bears blot out the field as the big men stare past the conferring coaches. A jubilant fullback accepts a happy handshake as he returns to the sidelines after scoring on a long run or a long pass. This is the bench.

The Coaches

Along the sidelines the coaches stride, sometimes kicking at the dirt, often conferring with their quarterbacks, eternally seeking the one flaw, the small crack through which to strike. Stout Steve Owen (left), whose career spanned the four decades of professional football, was in his last game when this picture was taken, but the solemn look on his face was for the problem of the moment, not the end of his career. All the coaches' faces are intent: cool, calculating Paul Brown (top), ebullient Weeb Ewbank, his pupil (below), all.

Mud

The game goes on despite rain or snow or mud. Baseball players get a day off if it rains; the football player hunches his shoulders so that the back of his helmet will protect his neck from the cold wet, and plays. Mud is not, really, an equalizer; the better team wins in the mud as it would win on a dry field. A Steve Van Buren runs for 196 yards in a championship game as the Philadelphia Eagles beat the Los Angeles Rams 14-0 in a cloudburst (1949). "It doesn't hurt the passers," a defensive halfback says bitterly. "It hurts us. We have to be able to react fast. You try reacting in mud up to your ankles. The receiver knows where he's going. We can't move until he does. Mud murders defensive halfbacks." The field is covered by a tarpaulin before the game, but when the tarpaulin is rolled back, the rain softens the turf, and twenty-two big men, wearing the extra-long mud cleats they need for traction, quickly make the field a quagmire. The uniforms gradually turn black and only the colors of the bright, splattered helmets differentiate the teams. The rain capes cloak the line of players on the bench in anonymity, and the dirty, cold faces peer out from under them impassively. At every break in the game—a time-out or an injury or a measurement for a first down—the trainers scurry out on the field and scrape the mud from between the cleats on the players' shoes—backs and ends first, then linemen if there is time. But the game goes on . . . and on.

The last play uncoils sluggishly in the muck. The stands have emptied long since and the players on the bench are huddled listlessly against the rain. The crack of the officials' gun marking the end of the game echoes back from the empty seats glistening in the shine from the stadium lights turned on long ago to fight the gloom. The players get up slowly and trot heavily to the dressing room and a warm shower. The game itself may have meant nothing.

Training Camp

JULY is baseball and hot dogs and swimming pools and vacation time for most people. The sun hammers down like a white-hot sledge, and at night in New York and Chicago and Philadelphia the poor people cluster sweatily on the fire escapes and long for autumn and coolness.

In a dozen small towns across the United States, autumn has already come. Heat still shimmers on the flat green of the football fields, but the sound of autumn is there in the solid thump of a long punt and the rasp, clatter and thwack of big men battling in the armor of their trade. For the men who make up the rosters of the twelve professional football teams in the National Football League, the season has started. For some of them—the rookies who haven't the step of speed that makes the difference and the veterans who have lost it—the season will end quickly and sadly in a few weeks. For the good ones, it will stretch into the bitter cold of December.

But December is a long way off now. Training camp is the world, and it's a tough world, whose law is the survival of the fittest. A typical pro camp is located at a small college in a small town. The players sleep in one dormitory, eat at the college cafeteria, which is in operation early to take care of them. The food is simple and runs to steaks and roasts almost to the point of monotony. The days are long and hard, and few players object to the eleven-o'clock curfew. This is a business—a hard, demanding one—and these are businessmen with

no time now for frivolity. Sleep is an investment in energy which will be sorely needed the next day, and no one quarrels with the early bedtime.

The day starts at 7:00, breakfast at 7:30. On the field at 9:30, hard, grueling practice until 11:00, then lunch from 12:00 to 1:00. The early afternoon is spent in meetings, with the offensive and defensive units separate, then back to the field at 3:00 or 4:00 for two more hours of applying what was learned in the meetings. Dinner comes at 6:00 or 7:00 and there's usually another meeting from 8:00 to 10:00. Then an hour to write home or play cards or listen to the lonesome sound of a record player singing the same song over and over again down the hall. (For some reason, most rookies play one record interminably. That's how "Night Train" Lane, the Cardinal defensive halfback, got his nickname.)

The Turk makes his rounds in that last hour of the long day. The Turk is an assistant coach whose unpleasant duty it is to end the dreams of a rookie or the career of a veteran. He finds the player alone and tells him quietly, almost furtively, that he is through. Some players listen stoically, some plead for another chance, some curse, but all of them leave. They go on an early train or plane and they are driven into town in the gray of morning, before breakfast. No one likes a ghost at table with him. The players check the chow line every morning, the guards counting guards, tackles counting tackles, ends, ends. The line grows short as camp nears its end, and the fit, who have survived, eat heartily.

The Ordeal of the Rookie

THEY COME in levis and Ivy League suits, buckskin shoes and cowboy boots. They talk in the soft, slurred syllables of the South and in the nasal twang of New England. They are brash, bashful, quiet, loud, tall, short. All of them are strong and quick and very skillful at their trade, which is football. Their chance of continuing to practice that trade is small indeed, since usually only three or four of the thirty-odd rookies in a pro training camp manage to make the team.

Some of them are All-Americans, fresh from the best year of their lives. Others played on small-college teams, before small crowds, and the big city is a new experience and a frightening one. All of them, in the democracy of the training camp where last year's clippings are less than meaningless, start afresh in a game vastly more complex and confusing than the one they played in college.

The typical rookie comes from a major college. He was a fine player there; he wouldn't be in this training camp otherwise. He was a campus figure and nearly everyone knew him and he was, naturally, sensible of his own importance. Now he is a stranger in a new land and he suits up in the dressing room with the other rookies. Maybe he's a back, and he looks furtively at the other backs while he dresses. They're big, he thinks. God, they're big. He's a little sick at the stomach from nerves and he and the other rookies dress silently while the old pros chat easily and talk about summer jobs and girls and the season coming and the season past and girls. They ignore the rookies and when the team clatters out of the dressing room to the practice field, the rookies walk together and the veterans walk in the small groups that the years have formed.

IN THE first scrimmage, the rookie finds out that the pros are even bigger and faster and tougher than he had feared. The noise in the line comes as a shock; the big men curse and shout and groan, and the pop of leather on leather is a fearsome thing. And there's no quarter shown to rookies. The veterans are fighting for their jobs, too, and they fight with guile and power. It is not enough to be strong and brave and quick; everyone on this team is. There's a plus quality of toughness of mental fiber and mental agility which makes the final difference.

The trial period, for the best of the rookies, lasts nearly two months, through some six exhibition games. These games are not the less for being ex-hibitions; the players on both teams are earning their right to stay for the regular league season and they hit hard. Once the teams used to play intrasquad games; most of them have quit that now because the intrasquad games were blood baths in which the bitter intramural battle for existence led to violence and injury. Failure for a rookie is absolute. No matter how often he tells himself and his friends, when he gets back home, that an assistant coach disliked him or that he wasn't given a chance, he knows that he was tried fairly by his betters and found lacking.

FOR THE rookie who makes the team, a new trial begins. Mistakes which were condoned in practice or in exhibition games draw quick and bitter censure now from teammates and from coaches. Now the games count in dollars and cents, and now the erstwhile rookie is a man among men and he is expected to perform as one. The arsenal of plays which arms a pro team on offense or defense is staggering, and it takes long hours of study for the rookie to master assignments which have become second nature to the old pros on the team. Then there are the technical subtleties of football—the techniques of blocking and tackling and running which college coaches lacked the time or the knowledge to explain. There is, too, the never-ending study of the personnel of the other teams, the sure knowledge of which defensive halfback commits himself too quickly on a running play, which end covers the outside well but can't close the gap between himself and the tackle. The rookie learns, by bruising experience, never to loaf, never to relax. He learns never to stand and look at the pile when a ball carrier is down, because then he is an easy target for a shattering block. The safe place is on top of the pile, and if the unknowledgeable fans howl at him for piling on, he knows his fellow players understand.

He becomes a member of a team within a team. For a while, he'll probably play on the suicide squad —the special team which kicks off or receives the kickoff. Eventually, as time and injuries wear away the starting offensive and defensive platoons, he'll earn a place on one of them. He'll find that, if he's on the defensive platoon, his friends will be defensive players and he'll be part of the defensive *esprit de corps*. A pro football team is two teams, separate and distinct, with different coaches, different skills, different things to learn.

As the year declines into December, he'll find he's no longer a rookie, except in name. His education as a pro is still far from complete; it may never be really complete, and in the season five or six years away when he hangs up his jock strap, he may feel, as many old pros feel, that he is quitting just as he is truly learning how to play football.

By the season's end, he is tougher and stronger and probably — because pro football rookies start their careers young, while they are still growing —bigger. When he goes back to the small town where he was raised, he'll be different—sure of himself, because he has made it in the most demanding sport in the world. And next year he'll look at the rookies coming up tolerantly, but he won't remember how it felt.

Work Books and Film

THE Bible of the pro player is a loose-leaf notebook provided him by the head coach. In it is distilled all the knowledge essential to the proper prosecution of his assignments. It's not an easy book to master; some pro teams have as many as 300 offensive plays (see sample page at right), and none of these plays will work perfectly unless every man on the field performs his duty at least minimally. Each play sheet describes the duties of each man on every play. During the season, depending on how well the play works against the various defenses in the league, changes are made by the coaches. The variations are entered in each workbook. The book is a valuable property; when a player is traded or cut, his book is picked up, and the loss of the book can cost, in fines, as much as $300. The book is for home study and for notes; at player meetings, as often as not, the player

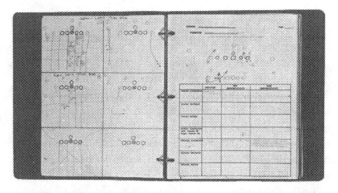

studies movies. He watches, on a wide screen, the team and the player he will face the next week, searching for minute flaws, for telltale patterns of behavior. And, uncomfortably, he watches himself in action while the coaches go over in painful detail his sins of omission or commission.

Here's the difference in the picture you see on your television screen (inset area) and the one that players and coaches study in preparation for a game to come or in criticizing a game past. The wide-screen camera used in scouting film is designed to encompass all 22 players on each play.

Part Three

THE GAMES

THE EXHIBITIONS begin in the relentless heat of late summer. By the time the league season starts in September, the teams have been winnowed to the 35 men who will play together for twelve Sundays; the 35 men have been separated into offensive and defensive squads and they think of themselves as members of this team within a team. They settle into the routine of the season: play Sunday, off Monday, game movies, skull sessions, practice Tuesday through Friday, a light workout Saturday, play Sunday. The weeks roll by, one very much like another except that it gets colder and colder. But the games are all different—different problems, different stratagems, a different feel and flavor each Sunday afternoon. The stadiums are biased battlefields; every team prefers the familiar confines of its own park. The veterans come to know the *querencias* of the enemy: the windy, cold confines of Wrigley Field, where the Chicago Bears fans are so close to the bench that sometimes, in the late stages of a game, they sit with the players and jeer at them. They know Kezar Stadium in San Francisco, where the gulls and the fog sweep in from the bay as the sun sets. The massive cement oval of the Coliseum in Los Angeles can be a sweat bath in the early months of the season; the temperature on the floor of the big bowl is often ten degrees hotter than anywhere else in the city, and no breeze finds its way there from the ocean twenty miles away. In Baltimore, the big crowds are loud and fiercely partisan, and after every Colt touchdown a young lady gallops around the football field on a cream-colored pony, falling off once or twice a season. The towering green walls of Yankee Stadium remind the rookies of Ruth and Gehrig and DiMaggio, but to the veterans they mean early long shadows laying damp coldness over the field, and the early turning on of the stadium lights. The punt returners learn, in time, to play the wind which funnels through Cleveland's Municipal Stadium, blowing cold off Lake Erie just beyond the open end of the stands. Pittsburgh, Philadelphia, Detroit, Green Bay—in each city the park and the fans who inhabit it lend their own peculiar flavor to the game, but the games themselves, by virtue of the time of the season and the personnel and the importance in the league standings, develop their own special characters. The early games are probings and testings to discover what has changed since last year and how good the rookies are and how old the veterans have grown. Later, the testing is over and the problem is fairly put and the teams take the field knowing very well the difficulty of the task ahead. As the season wanes, the race in each division narrows to two or three teams, but, oddly enough, the teams which are virtually out of contention still play with the fierce pride which marks pro football. The difference between first and last place in a division may have turned on a matter of inches in a few games: a first-down attempt inches short, a pass inches too long, a field goal inches too wide. The players know this and live with the bitter knowledge that this was not their year, not because of any lack of skill or strength but because the gods of football smiled on someone else at the crucial moments. So they play the leaders violently to prove their own excellence, and the teams are so closely matched that, often enough, the last-place team wallops the champion. No outcome is impossible. Sunday after Sunday, the battle is a new one, and a chance for glory.

The Sudden Death Classic: *New York-Baltimore*
YANKEE STADIUM, NEW YORK, DECEMBER 28, 1958

The West: *San Francisco-Los Angeles*
KEZAR STADIUM, SAN FRANCISCO, OCTOBER 4, 1959

The Midwest: *Chicago-Detroit*
WRIGLEY FIELD, CHICAGO, DECEMBER 13, 1959

The East: *New York-Cleveland*
YANKEE STADIUM, NEW YORK, DECEMBER 6, 1959

The 1959 Championship: *Baltimore-New York*
BALTIMORE MEMORIAL STADIUM, DECEMBER 27, 1959

The Sudden Death Classic

The 1958 championship game between the New York Giants and the Baltimore Colts, in Yankee Stadium, was, quite simply, the best football game ever played. It matched two superb football teams in the most important game of the year. Often, in a game so tense, one or the other of the teams will play poorly; in this case, both teams played magnificently. This game had long runs, long passes and heart-stopping defensive stands by both teams. But other championship games have had all of that. The fact that in this game, for the first time in football history, the sudden-death ruling went into effect added the final fillip which made it the best ever. With two minutes to play, the Giants led 17-14. They missed a first down by inches and elected to punt rather than try again on fourth down. It was a logical decision; in Don Chandler the Giants have the best punter in the business and the Giant defense is one of the two best. But they did not reckon with the cool nerve of John Unitas. With the clock moving inexorably, Unitas led his team nearly the length of the field, throwing with devastating accuracy when he had to, picking minute flaws in the Giant running defense when he found them. With twelve seconds left, Steve Myhra kicked a field goal and the game went into a sudden-death overtime. The team scoring first won the game and the Giants had the first chance. This was a gallant Giant team which had beaten the Cleveland Browns three games in a row, including a playoff game for the division championship, to reach this cold afternoon. They tried mightily but they were a tired team, shocked by the devastating drive the Colts had made for the game-tying field goal. They were forced to punt, and Unitas came back at them again. Under the incredible pressure of the moment, both teams played crisp, intelligent and nearly perfect football. But the Colts had too much. The big Colt offensive line, led by Jim Parker (77 to the right, shown obliterating the Giants' Andy Robustelli), gave Unitas an impenetrable wall of blockers and he sent his wonderful receivers—Raymond Berry, Lennie Moore and Jim Mutscheller—sifting into the Giant secondary time and again for key passes. With a first down inside the Giant ten, Unitas crossed up the Giants, the press box and the stands by throwing a flat pass to Jim Mutscheller. Asked why he took this gamble, he said, "I don't expect interceptions when I throw." With a sure field goal in hand, he gambled again and sent Ameche crashing over for the winning score.

The Elixir: Unitas to Berry

Here is the classic picture of the one weapon which, more than any other, accounted for the Giants' downfall. Raymond Berry (82) caught twelve passes in this game. He caught them despite the fact that the Giants nearly always devoted two defenders to him. Here Unitas has fired at the precise moment that Berry has gained the half-step he needs to have a clear shot at the ball. This is a simple hook pass, designed to gain enough yardage for a first down. Berry started straight downfield, feinted toward the sideline to make the halfback take one step in that direction, then suddenly curled back to the middle of the field, toward the line of scrimmage. The step in the wrong direction has left the halfback powerless to stop the pass; the linebacker, barely visible in front of Berry, has his back turned to the play, covering the flaring fullback, Ameche. Nevertheless, the ball has to be thrown with pinpoint accuracy; if it is off target appreciably, one of the two Giant defenders will be in position to bat it down or intercept it. It is this wonderful, intuitive communication between Unitas and Berry that makes them nearly unstoppable.

Unitas' cool disregard for danger shows in this picture in which he has just thrown the ball. Berry (82) is open downfield and the ball is on target although Unitas must have known as he released it that Huff would clobber him immediately. Unitas has an exceptionally quick delivery so that he can wait until the last possible second to unload; in this case, as in many others, that ability to wait plus the daring to use it resulted in a pass completion. The extra time gives Unitas' receivers more room to maneuver, and a receiver like Berry, who is one of the best fakers in the game, is almost sure to get free.

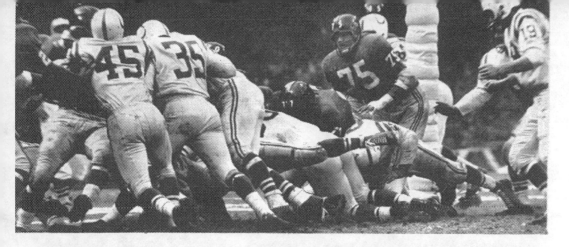

Early in the third period the Giants, battered and reeling under the magnificent assault of the Colts, suddenly rallied. Four times the great Giant defense turned back Baltimore inside the 3-yard line.

The Giants caught fire, went ahead. With two minutes to go they needed only this first down to win. Gifford (16) swung wide cut back and was hit by Lipscomb and Marchetti inches short. Marchetti broke his ankle

Now, with time of the essence (right), Unitas directed a flawless drive from his 18. Three times, nervelessly, he threw to Raymond Berry. The third time put the ball on the Giant 1½ with seconds left.

Here the most important field goal in pro history is up and away. All the players, Giants and Colts, and all the fans are watching as the 20-yard kick slices narrowly through the goal posts. Time left: 7 seconds.

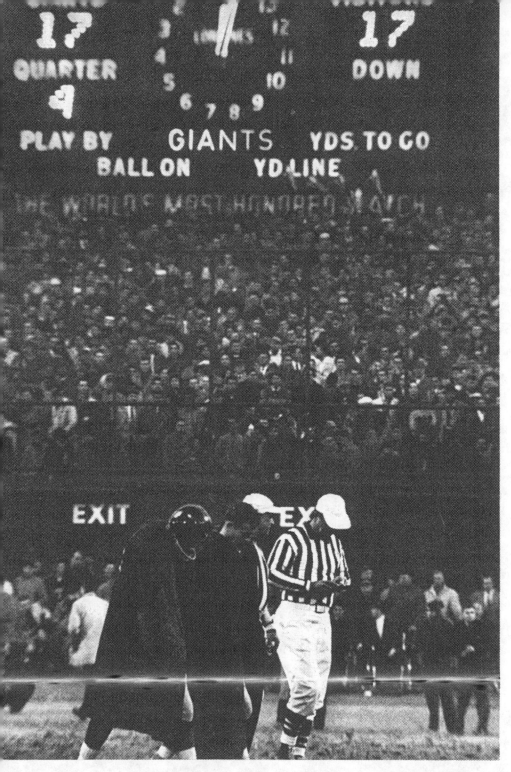

Now, for the first time in all football history, a championship will be decided in a sudden-death overtime. The officials and team captains walk down the field for the toss of the coin which will start the overtime and decide who receives. The scoreboard records the moment indelibly. Fittingly, this was the last game recorded by this scoreboard; a new electronic marvel replaced it in 1959.

The Sudden Death Overtime

The Giants received and, again, were denied victory by inches. A pass to Schnelker was inches wide; Conerly, unable to find a receiver, ran on third down and, churning valiantly on 37-year-old legs, was turned aside violently on a driving tackle by backers Pellington and Shinnick.

133

Now the Colts took over. Each play was freighted with almost unbearable tension, but Baltimore played steadily, coolly, inexorably. With 3rd and 15, Unitas (above) was given magnificent protection by the Colt line. Taking his time, he looked first at Lennie Moore, the intended receiver, saw he was covered. He then rolled out wide all alone and looked for Berry, saw the defensive halfback covering him slip, and calmly motioned to Berry to go deeper. Only then, sure of the first down, did Unitas throw to Berry. On the next play, a trap (below) sent Ameche (35) bulling straight ahead for 23 yards, to within easy field-goal range. "We trapped Modzelewski," Unitas said later. "He was blowing in there on me too fast."

With first and goal to go on the Giant 8, Unitas sent Ameche into the middle (left). Ameche cut back directly over center when he thought he saw daylight there, but Sam Huff (70) closed the hole and momentarily delayed disaster.

The play that won the game below started out precisely the same as the one above, but this time Ameche headed straight off the right tackle. The key to the play was the mighty block that Mutscheller put on Cliff Livingston (89), who is shown reaching for the fullback with a desperate, helpless hand. So ended the best football game ever played.

The West:

San Francisco and Los Angeles

In this game, played at Kezar Stadium in the amber afternoon light of early fall in northern California, Red Hickey, coach of the 49ers, devised and brought off a defensive miracle. The Rams, with the most explosive offensive talent in the league, had crushed the 49ers two weeks earlier; on this day, they were stopped as cold as any football team has ever been.

The old men of the 49er offense carried the attack: eagle-bald Y.A. Tittle (14) hands off to Hugh McElhenny.

Below, big Leo Nomellini (73), one of the best defensive tackles in the game, drives in on fast Billy Wade (9).

Fullback Joe Perry (34), whose uniform number tells his age, follows the violent blocking for a long 49er gain.

But it was the defense which keyed and established the dominance of the 49ers over the Rams all afternoon.

The young, fast 49er secondary blanketed the great Ram receivers; here (above) Eddie Dove bats away a pass which was intercepted by another 49er defensive back coming up fast. The red jerseys of the 49ers ringed the Ram receivers all day, and the 49er tackling was hard, sure and positive, as on Tom Wilson (right).

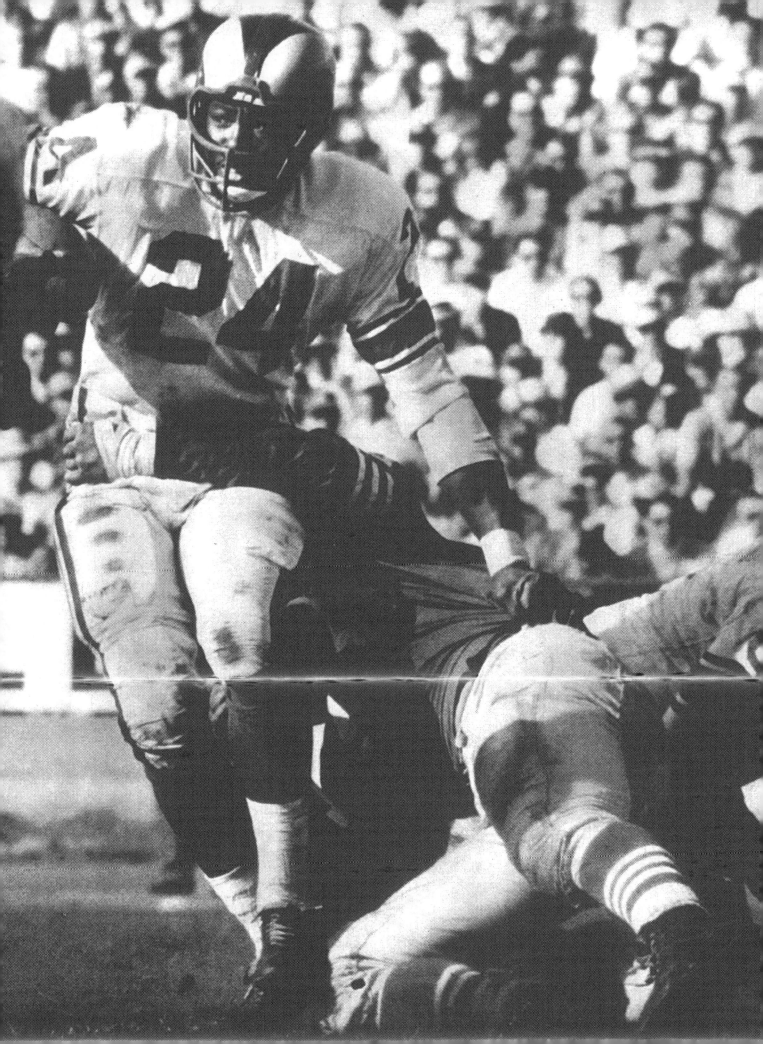

A Memorable Sunday Afternoon

No one but the 49er coach, Red Hickey, and the 49ers themselves believed they could beat the Rams. As the game ended, the late Bert Bell, commissioner of the league, called the press box from Philadelphia to get the score. Told "34-0, San Francisco," he barked, "Don't kid me, young man. I'm the commissioner of this league." It took a while to convince Bell that the score really was 34-0; it took a while for the 49ers themselves to realize it. Hickey, in his first year as a head coach, had gambled brilliantly on the ability of his young, antelope-fast defensive backs to cover the fine Ram receivers man on man. Abe Woodson (left) typifies the adhesive quality of the 49er pass defense; he covered Del Shofner (29) step for step on all of the intricate Ram pass patterns. On the other side of the line, Jerry Mehrtens took Red Phillips, and the two deep men, rookies Eddie Dove and Dave Baker, played like veterans. The line was magnificent but these young men were unbelievable.

Below, the game is over and the crowd stands happily under the scoreboard while the players move off slowly.

A Bear linebacker (61) and a Detroit tackle brace for the jolting man-to-man collision which makes pro football.

The Midwest:

Chicago and Detroit

This game between the Chicago Bears and the Detroit Lions, played in the cold confines of Wrigley Field near the end of the season, had no effect on the standings. Both teams were out of the race and the Lions were ending one of the worst seasons in the history of the club. The Bears were trying for their seventh straight victory, but the Baltimore Colts were already champions of the West. Wrigley Field was full. The picture on the next page shows the faces of the Bear fans; the late, chill light of the December sun rings them with a pale halo. The fans are bundled against the bitter weather, but their enthusiasm is warm as ever. These are an older order of fans than the ones who sat in sun-filled Kezar Stadium to watch the 49ers play the Rams; some of them are sitting in seats they inherited from their parents. The game — violent, dramatic — is the same.

The Bears won the game. The score makes little difference; this was a truly typical pro game, filled with the big plays and the excitement of the sport. Above, Ed Brown (15) throws a screen pass over the Lions.

Below, big Ed McColl, the medical student who plays end for the Bears, sets off with the pass en route to one of the touchdowns which gave the Bears a long lead at the half. It dwindled in the last half.

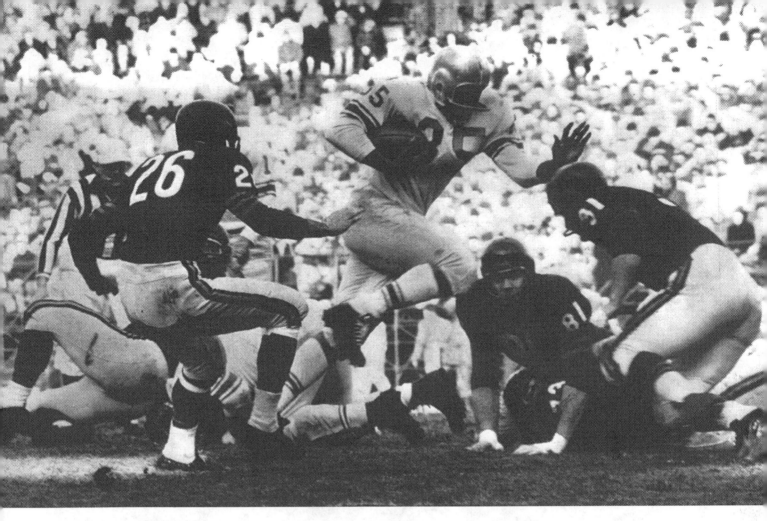

John Henry Johnson, a very big, very fast fullback who has been around a long time, threads his way through the Bears, on a long run in the second half. Johnson had been having a bad year until this game.

The Lion second-half passing attack fell short, despite a great catch by Terry Barr (41) and a great try by Dave Middleton (84). It was Homecoming Day for former Bears and they came and stayed and cheered.

George Halas, who owns the Bears and coaches them and who has been in professional football since its beginnings 40 years ago, rests his arm affectionately on the shoulder of his first great T quarterback, Sid Luckman. There are only minutes remaining now and the game is won and George is happy about it, but he's looking ahead to next year. The Bears have won their seventh straight to close out another season, and Halas and Luckman, now a Bear assistant coach, are happy.

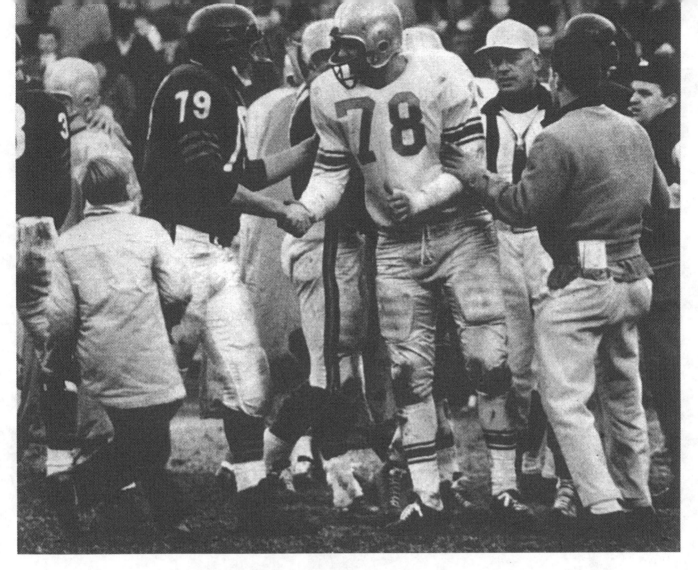

After the Battle

The game—and the season—is over and the two linemen above will hang up the stained armor of their trade for seven months. The violence and bitterness of their dueling on the field is forgotten, as indeed it is usually forgotten after each game. The old pros seldom carry grudges; they take the inevitable battering and the occasional injuries of their business with good grace. "You can't afford to take out personal grudges on the field," one player said recently. "While you're trying to get somebody on the other team, you can't play your position properly. You're hurting your club and eventually, when contract-signing time comes, you'll find you're hurting yourself. So you forget it. If you want to stay in the league, you forget it." The real prototype of the old pro, Pittsburgh quarterback Bobby Layne, demonstrated the veteran's attitude perfectly in an exhibition game with the Bears in Miami. The Bears got through Bobby's blockers and four big defenders buried the blond Texan under a gang tackle. He lay quietly under a thousand pounds of Bears and waited until they slowly peeled off him. As the last one got up, Bobby scrambled to his feet. In his oddly high-pitched Texas drawl he said, "Hey, fellows. We're having a party at Joe's tonight. Come on over." Of course, there are some feuds in the league. Once Bob Waterfield of the Rams and Ed Sprinkle, the legendary end of the Chicago Bears and one of the meanest ends ever to play, traded broken jaws over two seasons. Charley Trippi, the old Cardinal halfback, ended the season one year by calmly walking over to Sprinkle in the waning seconds of the last game and belting him with a roundhouse right. Sprinkle crumpled and Trippi trotted off the field happily. "It was worth it," he said when he paid his fine. But usually the handshake at the end of a game is a sincere one. These are, after all, men with a common trade and a dangerous one, and this particular community of interests welds them into a tight-knit, exclusive fraternity—the fraternity of courage.

The East:

New York and Cleveland

Each game in the twelve—now thirteen—Sundays of the season has its own flavor, its own excitement. In this one, between the powers of the East, the Giant defensive coach, Tom Landry, answered all the questions put by the very strong Cleveland offense. At left, the Brown big gun, Jim Brown, is snowed under by three Giant defenders: Jim Patton (20), Dick Nolan (25) and ubiquitous Sam Huff (70).

Masterpiece by Twelve Defensemen

The little Dutch boy who saved his town by putting his finger in a hole in the dike had a simple job compared to a modern pro defense. The holes in the dike outnumber the fingers available to plug them; it is rarely that a defense is able to stop a pro offense as thoroughly as the Giant defenders did in this game. It was a twelve-man defense; in short yardage situations, the Giants substituted massive Rosey Brown (79), an offensive tackle, to lend beef to the line. Above, the powerful Rosey splits his blockers as the ball is barely in the fullback's hand to stop the Brown inside running cold. Below, the agile Jim Katcavage tackles the fleet Bobby Mitchell as he tries to skirt the Giant flank. Top left, Giant tackle Rosy Grier goes up to block off a Plum pass, and bottom left, a Cleveland tackle (74) measures the narrow difference between success and, in this case, failure.

153

The Relentless Attack

The Giant offensive team, smarting under sharp criticism for weeks, blew the Browns off the field, scoring over a point a minute the first three quarters. They scored quickly and easily: Gifford, above, alone to catch a touchdown pass; Rote, below, leaving a scattered trail of Browns as he tumbles into the end zone with another pass; and Webster (left) climbing high under the pendant raindrops on the crossbar to take still another touchdown pass and run the score to 48-0. Still it wasn't enough for the hungry Giant offense. An hour after the game, in a Giant dressing room deserted by everyone else, guard Jack Stroud sat tensely, pounding his fists on the bench and saying regretfully, "We didn't score enough!"

Through the cold of a snowy December afternoon, two youngsters scamper gleefully the length of the football field with a policeman in futile pursuit. The big crowd in Yankee Stadium, happy enough over the shellacking they have watched their beloved Giants hand to the Cleveland Browns to win the Eastern Division championship, roared encouragement to these two boys, who finally escaped with their football. The crowd then poured down out of the stands in uncontrollable enthusiasm, invaded the field before the game ended and tore down the goal posts while Cleveland Coach Paul Brown led his charges to the safety of the dressing room. It was the end of a glorious comeback for the Giants, who won five straight as the season ended, then looked to Baltimore.

Practice and Planning

On the same field a few days later, the Giants begin meticulous preparation for the championship game. The stands are empty and the two boys have retired somewhere to a vacant lot to play with the ball they acquired so spectacularly. The players, clad in sweat suits, begin the infinitely precise choreography of football, tracing plays over and over again on the brown dead grass of Yankee Stadium. The field is like a rehearsal area for an invasion, with the coaches translating their scouting reports on the Baltimore Colts into a plan of attack, then drilling the troops endlessly in the execution of the plan. The coaching staff spends hours every day in going over movies of the Baltimore team in action, searching for a flaw in the Colt defense or a telltale giveaway by an offensive player which may tip the Giant defense to a play. From the hours of study come the strategy and tactics of this miniature warfare, and, finally, the staff decisions are translated in checks and circles on a blackboard, the shorthand of football. In Baltimore, the Colts are synthesizing their strategy.

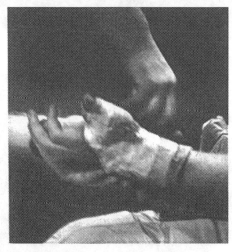

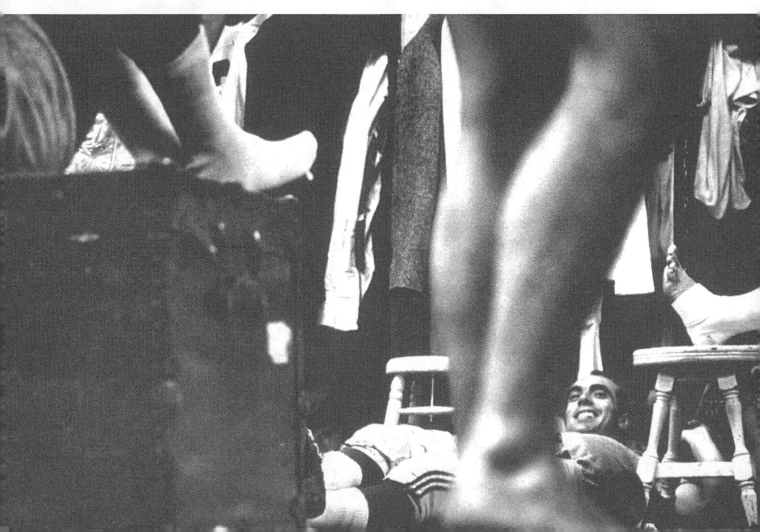

The tense quiet before battle prevails in the Giant dressing room. A player tightens his cleats, an owner looks over the program, not seeing it. An offensive tackle rechecks his assignment, and Defensive Coach Tom Landry tells Rosy Grier, "On goal-line defense, remember to charge low and straighten up the blocker." Hands are bandaged and the ready players relax and wait. Charlie Conerly, a veteran of the wars, is girded yet again to go forth into combat, the trainer wrapping aging ankles tenderly. And on a table the doctor's kit is open and ready against the time soon to come when it will be needed.

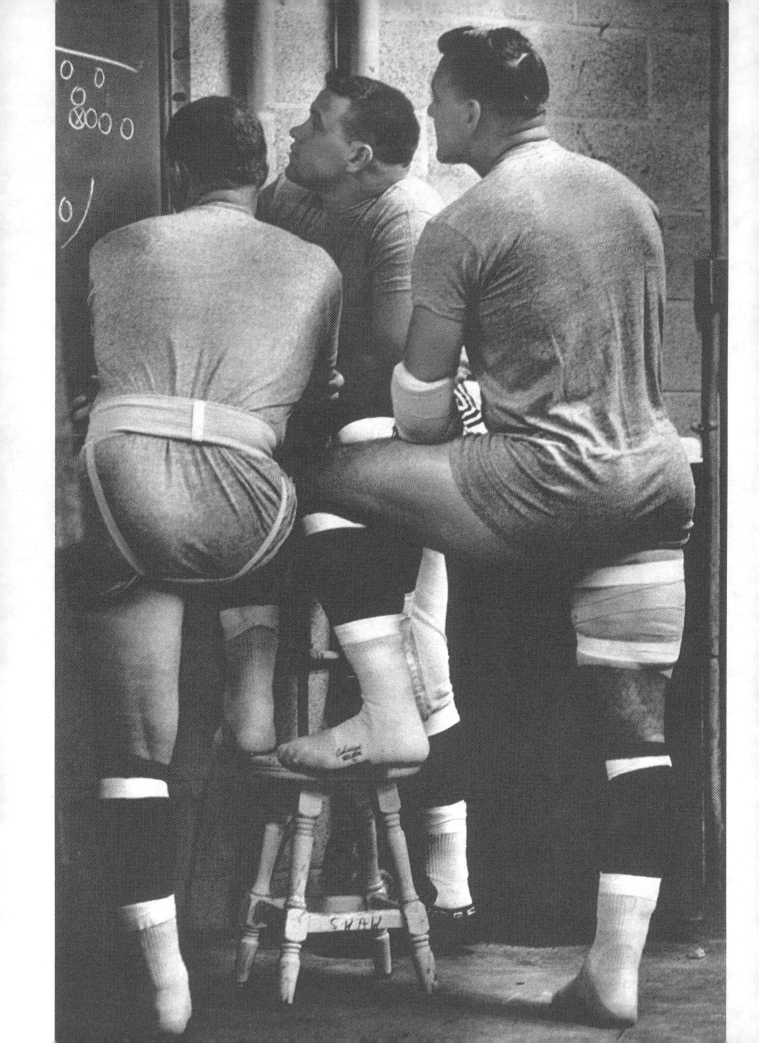

The units gather in small groups to go over, for the last time, their assignments. Before the blackboard, tackle Dick Modzelewski and a couple of other defenders study the circles and X's of their trade and try to guess what the Colts will do to upset their calculations. They talk in quick shorthand, incomprehensible to strangers—"Blitz Wanda, blitz Meg"—war terms for the miniature war waiting.

Strapped and taped and needing only to put on the heavy armor plate of the pads and uniforms, Kyle Rote makes a point on the first play the Giants will run, while back coach Allie Sherman and halfback Frank Gifford listen intently. The year and the season and the week and the day have dwindled down to this—one play which, if the Giants have planned well and are lucky, could establish the pattern of victory over the Colts.

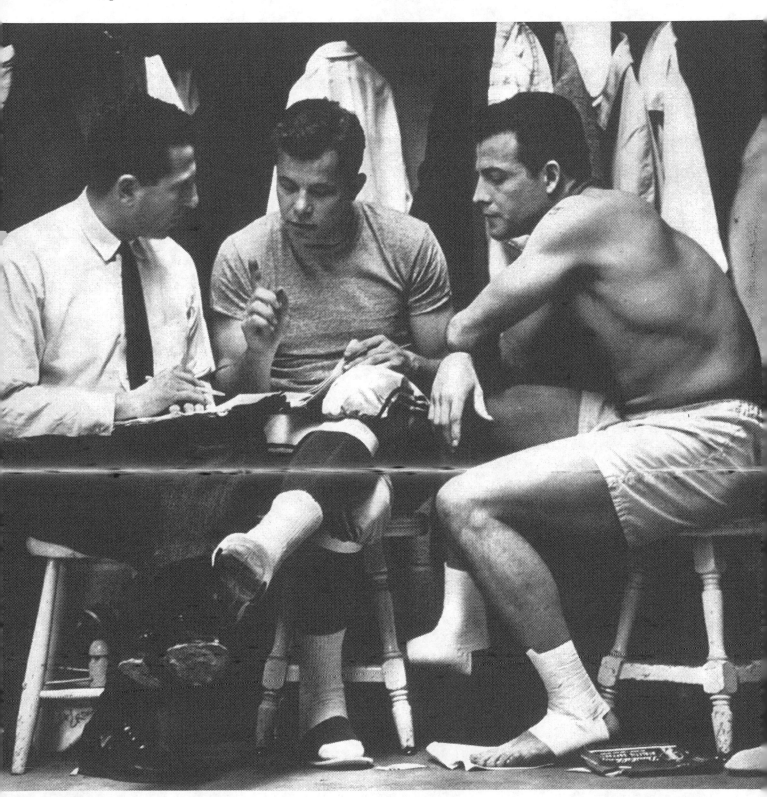

The *1959* Championship

Baltimore and New York

A Game of Momentum

Football is a game of momentum. The team which can establish and maintain momentum wins. The Giants, trying to get off to a fast start, nearly succeeded. The first play, which Sherman and Rote and Gifford went over so carefully in the dressing room just before the game began, was a pass to Rote. Flanked far to the left, Rote sliced across the Colt secondary to the right sideline, and Conerly's pass found him there. Unfortunately the throw was a bit short and the end had to slow down for the catch. With no room to maneuver, he could not turn for the goal line but was forced immediately to step out of bounds. As it was, the play gained 20 yards and then Gifford ran beautifully for 22 and it looked as if the Giants had established the momentum they wanted. But the big, brutal Colt line you see below, getting into gear more slowly than the Giants, began to take over and inexorably reversed the flow of the game. It was not apparent this early in the game. The Giants still moved the ball fairly well, but their gains grew shorter and shorter and harder to get.

1

The play with which the Colts established the initiative began with a reverse pivot by Unitas. It began on the Colt 40, after the first Giant drive had been stopped; it went all the way.

2

As Unitas faked this pitchout, the Giant linebackers on this side started to the right. Berry, the intended receiver (82), went straight down at Lynch; on the other side, Moore (24) took off.

3

Now Unitas watches as Berry slants in with the Giants' Lynch and Svare covering him. The defensive strategy was designed to cover Berry with two men, gamble with one man on Moore.

4

Unitas cocks his arm to throw as Berry gains a step on Lynch, who came up slowly. Had Unitas thrown, he might have completed this pass for a short gain, but this was not the play.

5

Unitas completes the fake throw. As Berry cuts sharply to the sideline, he pulls Patton with him, and the Giant defense has spent three men defending against one —an error that proved fatal.

6

Unitas is still watching Berry as he nears the sidelines with Svare, Lynch and Patton moving in on him. Although there is no chance now of hitting Berry, Unitas feints a pass yet again.

7

So good is this feint that, incredibly, all of the Giant defense except Lindon Crowe is turned toward Berry, with their backs to Moore, on the other flank of the Baltimore Colt attack.

8

Now, in a flash, Unitas swings to the other side and sees Moore break free from Crowe. Nolan, the Giant safetyman on that side, ineptly has kept his back turned to Moore to watch Berry.

9

The play is three seconds old and Unitas is still under no pressure from the Giant line as he watches Moore pick up two steps on Crowe, cutting in toward the middle of the field.

10

The trap is sprung and Unitas prepares to fire. Nolan is trying desperately to recover and help Crowe, but the split second he lost in turning to watch the play on the other side is too much.

11

At this moment, Nolan might still have made the tackle on Moore after the pass was completed, but he made another mistake by turning the wrong way. He should have turned right.

12

Instead, he turned a complete circle to his left, and Moore, all out, took the pass and fled by the slowed-down Nolan. Moore was two steps ahead of Crowe when he caught the pass.

13
Bombs away now, just over desperate finger tips of Giant end Andy Robustelli, at last free of his blocker. Moore caught this perfectly thrown pass in full stride and no Giant had a chance to catch him (next page).

Failure Inside the Five

The massive Colt line underlined its mastery of the Giants late in the first period. Conerly had found a slight gap in a Baltimore defense, which was set up to deny the Giants running room outside the flanks, and he sent his fullback, Mel Triplett, booming up the middle for 28 yards. The Giants, briefly, appeared to have regained the initiative in the game. Triplett's long run put them on the Colt 16, and then Triplett gained six up the still vulnerable Colt middle and Conerly flipped a quick pass to big Bob Schnelker for four more yards and a first down on the Colt 6-yard line. There the momentum of the Giant drive halted. Conerly sent Alex Webster, the tough, hard-running Giant halfback,

into the line (left), and Big Daddy Lipscomb, the elephantine but agile Colt all-pro tackle, stopped him dead. Then Conerly went to the air and tossed a quick pass to Gifford wide to the right. Colt linebacker Bill Pellington (36, below) came up very fast and Gifford reversed his field and wheeled back to the left. The very quick, very alert Colt defenders moved with him, and when Gifford tried to turn upfield, he ran into the nest of defenders shown in the picture at the bottom of the page. He lost six yards on this completed pass, and on the next play Conerly, dropping back to pass again, lost seven yards. The Giants then called on Pat Summerall and settled for a field goal.

Harried by the consistent, violent attack of the Colt defensive line, Conerly often had to run for his life (above). Still, he managed to get his passes away despite the duress he labored under. The completions, like this one to Schnelker, below, came harder and harder as the battering took its toll of the Giant quarterback.

Ten Inches

Toward the end of the third period, the Colt line turned the tide of this game irrevocably against the Giants. New York, moving painfully and mostly via passes, had taken the lead, 9-7, on Pat Summerall's third field goal. A short Colt punt set them up on their own 44 and the Giant rooters who had followed the team to Baltimore began to chant, "Go, Giants, go!" A 19-yard pass to Gifford moved the Giants to the Colt 38 and a 10-yard third-down pass to Schnelker made it fourth down and ten inches to go on the Colt 28. The problem—a universal one of gaining the very difficult short yardage or punting—was curiously similar to the third-and-inches situation in the championship game in 1958 when Conerly sent Gifford into the line and he failed, giving Baltimore possession of the ball with two minutes left. The Colts got a field goal in those two minutes that tied the game, then won in overtime. This time, Conerly sent Webster into the Colt line and he gained not an inch. ("He should have dived for it. He never left his feet," Otto Graham said later.) The Colts took possession and the last Giant bid died.

A knot of Colt defenders and officials gather around the ball as head linesman holds hands high, indicating margin of ten inches Giants need for first down.

Below are the faces of victory. These are the Baltimore fans, early in the fourth quarter when the turn of the tide has become very clear and certain. The Colts are on the move and the Giants are a tired, beaten team. The fans come expecting victory, as they did every Sunday of the season, and the victory of this team—their team—makes each of them a little stronger and a little bigger than he— or she — was before this wintry afternoon. They whistle and laugh and yell and clap and some of them—like the plump woman just to the right of upper center—only beam very happily at the world at large. These are the people who have made pro football—clerks, stenographers, bus drivers, laborers, executives, housewives, children. Most of them lead quiet lives and Sunday is the high spot of the week; the excitement of the game quickens them; the struggle animates them and the sudden, shifting panorama of conflict on the field below thrills them. In the monotony of their jobs there is small chance for this kind of magic. Inside this friendly stadium they find release in the long lifting burst of a Moore run or a Unitas-to-Berry pass. For two hours, the little people are as big as a pro tackle, as fast as a halfback, as daring as a quarterback. And for the rest of the week—for the rest of the year, after a game like this championship contest—they can say, "I was there" and pontificate on the errors the Giants made or the choices Unitas had. Look again at the faces below. Where else can you find such unalloyed happiness in so heterogeneous a group? Short, tall, fat, thin, black, white, young, old—all, for a couple of wonderful magic hours on a cold December afternoon, are one. For the victory being won on the field by the Baltimore Colts is not a victory of one football team over another; it is a victory over boredom and the disappointments of living for every Colt fan in the stands.

Two Key Passes

As the fourth quarter opened, these two passes—an unsuccessful one to Jim Mutscheller and a beautifully executed throw to Raymond Berry—set up the play which ended the Giant hopes. Mutscheller, the Colt right end, swung wide to his right on the first pattern. The Giant linebacker and defensive halfback on that side gave ground as he came downfield, and Mutscheller suddenly cut over center, between the two of them. Sam Huff, the Giant middle linebacker, had slid off a block to get in on Unitas, hurrying Johnny's throw, and the ball was just off Mutscheller's finger tips at the 50. But the play reinforced the Giant determination to cover Mutscheller with two men. On the next pass, the completion to Berry, Unitas underlined the necessity for covering Berry with two men, too. Berry was spread wide to the left, and, at the snap of the ball, he slanted in toward the center. Svare, the Giant linebacker, started to his right to cover a Colt halfback. He crossed in front of Lynch, who was covering Berry, and for a split second Svare screened Lynch's view of Unitas and the ball. In that split second Unitas threw and the ball was by Lynch before he could move to deflect it. Lynch reacted quickly, but Berry caught the pass for a 13-yard gain and a crucial first down for the Colts. On these two plays, Lennie Moore was covered by one Giant defender—Lindon Crowe. After trying a running play to pull in the Giant defense even more, Unitas triggered the trap so carefully set.

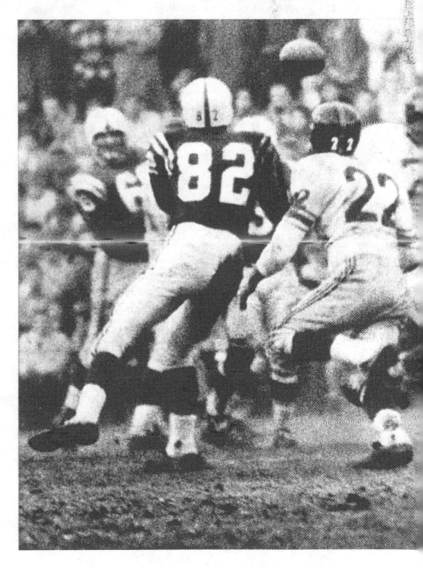

Moore's Run

In the grand strategy of Giant defense conceived by the brilliant young assistant coach, Tom Landry, Lennie Moore was conceded two touchdowns. "We give a team its strength," Landry explains. "Then we try to cut off everything else." This meant the Giants would assign one man—Lindon Crowe—the responsibility of covering Moore and accept the fact that Moore would likely get two touchdowns on Crowe. As the fourth period began, Moore had scored once. On this play, he just missed scoring, but he set up a touchdown, proving Landry a remarkably accurate prophet. The play was a simple one. Moore, flanked wide to the right, slanted sharply in at the snap of the ball, and Unitas, straightening up and throwing almost in one motion, hit him just over the line of scrimmage. Crowe was close as the pass was completed, and, but for an incredible bit of bad luck, he might have stopped the play for a short gain. Moore runs with the classic high knee action of nearly all great backs; as Crowe dived at his legs to make the tackle, Moore's knee came up and dealt him a crushing blow on the side of the head, knocking him out momentarily and leaving him dazed for the rest of the game. He fell off the tackle and Moore was away.

As the play gets under way (top), Unitas straightens up and snaps a quick pass to Moore (center) as Crowe hurries over to make the tackle. He appears to have Moore locked up (bottom) as he drives in.

Here Crowe has made contact; Moore's right knee catches him on the side of the head with numbing force.

As the beautifully balanced Moore drives on, Crowe falls to his hands and knees and Nolan (25) comes up fast to help out on the tackle. Giant linebacker Sam Huff is on the way at top speed.

Now Moore cuts very sharply to his left as Nolan and Huff close in. His amazing ability to move laterally without loss of speed makes him one of the most dangerous runners in football.

Huff has overrun the tackle, Nolan is unable to recover and Moore is free. Behind his churning feet you can see Crowe falling flat on his face, stunned by the blow from Moore's knee.

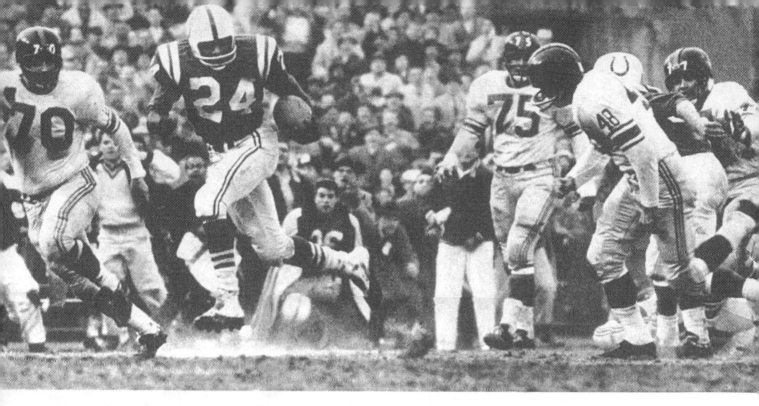

Moore is in the clear. He's moving very rapidly with the light, long stride which characterizes his running. Huff (70) trails him and Bill Stits has come over from the other side of the Giant defense.

Stits's diving tackle (below) slides off the twisting Moore but slows him so Lynch (22) can get to him and the doggedly pursuing Huff has time to assist in dragging the great Colt halfback to the ground.

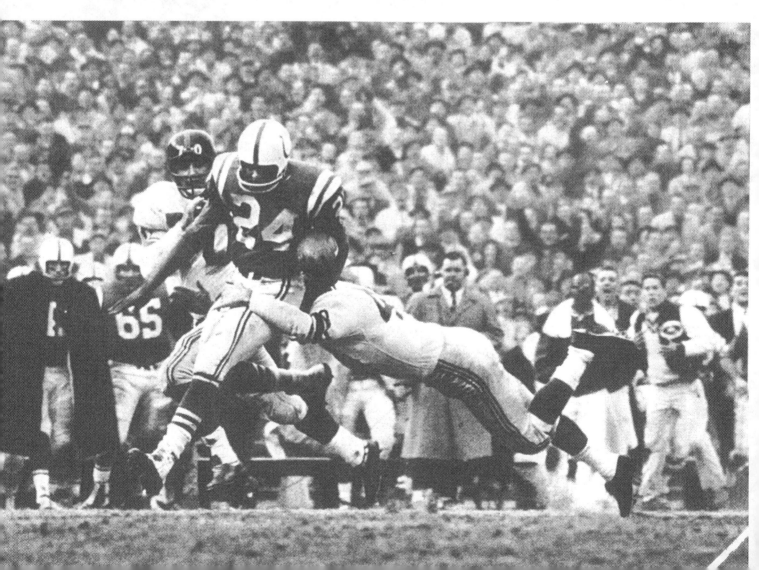

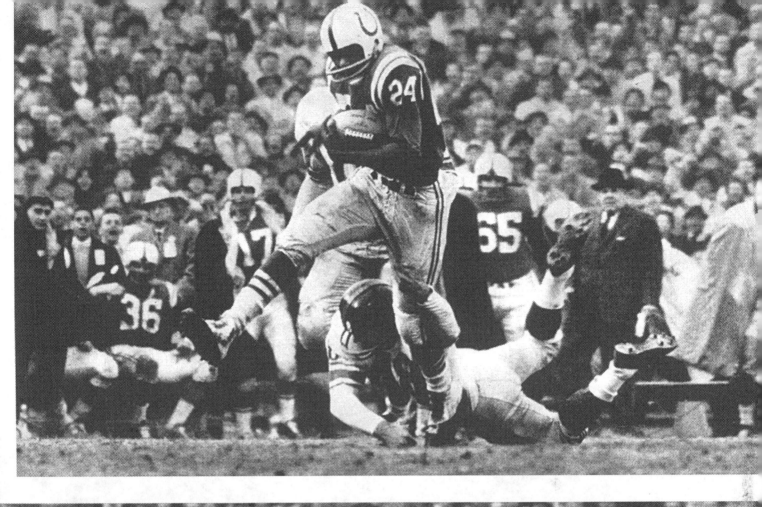

Pandemonium and the Ball Game

Moore's magnificent run carried to the Giant 14-yard line, covering 36 yards. Had Huff not trailed the play, Moore might have twisted away from Lynch (22) and fulfilled Landry's prophecy exactly. But as he spun away from Lynch (upper right), Huff bored in with a driving tackle to smash Moore to the turf (lower right). Three plays later, Unitas rolled out to his right, ostensibly to pass. When the dazed Crowe committed himself too soon in trying to cover Colt end Jim Mutscheller, Unitas ran the ball over for the touchdown which put the Colts ahead, 14-9, and which sealed the fate of the Giants. Trying desperately to regain the lead, the Giants, finding the big Colt line (next page) impervious to ground attack, resorted to the dangerous long pass, and the alert Colt secondary, spearheaded by cat-quick Johnny Sample, intercepted three times in quick succession. The loss of Jim

Patton in the second quarter and the injury to the still-dazed Crowe crippled the Giant defense. Unitas began throwing from a double wing formation, breaking his receivers into the open time and again. Had Patton been playing, the Giants might have gambled on his covering a Colt receiver alone; then they could have sent their linebackers crashing in on Unitas, forcing him out of the double wing attack. As it was, the Giant linebackers had to drop back to help the pass defenders, and Unitas coolly pinpointed his targets. The big crowd of Baltimore fans howled happily as Unitas passed 12 yards to rookie end Jerry Richardson for a touchdown. Sample intercepted a Conerly pass and returned it 42 yards for another, then set up a field goal with an interception of a pass thrown by Gifford. The Giants got a touchdown with 32 seconds to play, but all it changed was the final score, 31-16.

183

The Bright Future

THE QUIET YOUNG MAN on the opposite page is John Unitas, the architect of victory for the Baltimore Colts. When this picture was taken, Unitas was standing contentedly by the Baltimore bench as the clock ran out in the 1959 championship game. The victory was won and easily won, finally. A year before, he had stood in the closing seconds with his fists clenched, his face taut, watching his fullback churn through a gaping hole in the flank of the Giant defense to end the best football game ever played. Unitas is a young man who may, barring crippling injury, confidently expect another ten years as a quarterback. Professional football, as it enters its fifth decade, is an honorable profession, and to young men with the matchless ability of a Unitas or a Frank Gifford or a Jon Arnett it is an extremely profitable profession as well. Aside from the big paycheck to collect every Monday morning during the season, there are the perquisites of fame: endorsements, TV appearances, etc. Unitas and L. G. Dupre, a former teammate on the Colts, own a 48-lane, million-dollar bowling alley in Baltimore. Don Paul, who, as a linebacker for the Los Angeles Rams, once won the doubtful distinction of being the meanest man in pro football, is a prosperous and mellow restaurant owner in Los Angeles. Danny Fortmann, who was an all-pro guard for the Chicago Bears during their great years, is an eminent surgeon in Los Angeles; the Bears have another medic in training on the team in big Bill McColl, the giant end. Professional football for these men and for the many others like them is a steppingstone to security and success.

The teams which once traveled in ramshackle busses to play in tumbledown stadia before a handful of people now fly by jet planes to perform before crowds which sometimes exceed 100,000.

And this is only the beginning. The National Football League is expanding; a new franchise begins operation in Dallas in 1960 and another new club will start playing in Minneapolis–St. Paul, in 1961. For the second time since it began, the National Football League faces competition from a rival professional conference, too. The American Football League, founded by a young, enthusiastic and vastly wealthy Texan named Lamar Hunt, begins its schedule in 1960. Hunt, when he announced his new league, was snowed under with requests for franchises from all over the United States. The burgeoning interest in professional football is not confined to the twelve—now thirteen— cities with teams in the National Football League. The magic of television has carried the game into the smallest hamlets in the border states. The decade to come should see pro football take its place as America's true national sport.

Some of the old pros who sat on the running boards of the cars in a hot garage in Illinois long ago in the summer of 1920 and worked out the plan for the organization of the National Football League are still around. They were young men then, working out a way to remain young by playing a game they loved. Now they are bald or gray and, by the unrealistic measurement of years, they are old men. But if you watch George Halas on the sidelines at Wrigley Field, dancing with rage at what he considers an unfair penalty, or if you talk to him about the future of the Chicago Bears, you suddenly realize that this is the same man who wiped the sweat from his hand before he signed the first application for a franchise long ago in the garage in Cairo, Illinois. For this is a game for the young: young players, young coaches, young owners. It is a lusty, demanding game for a young, lusty and demanding nation.

The Names
and Numbers
of All
the Players

THE FOLLOWING *is a listing of all players not specifically identified in the text. The bold-face numbers refer to the page, visiting-team players are indicated as "w" (white jersey), and home-team players as "d" (dark jersey). In games prior to 1957, team initials are used (E = Eagles, G = Giants, etc.) because there was no league rule regulating jersey colors as there is today.*

Cover: 1958 Championship Game, Baltimore at New York, Yankee Stadium. d-70, Sam Huff; w-84, Jim Mutscheller; w-19, John Unitas; w-68, Alex Sandusky; d-77, Dick Modzelewski.
Endpapers: Fans at championship game, Baltimore Municipal Stadium, December 27, 1959.
Frontispiece: Kickoff; Pat Summerall, 88, New York Giants.

Part Two

28-29: Philadelphia at New York, Nov. 29, 1953. E-11, Bobby Thomason; G-51, Dick Woodard; E-67, John Magee; G-73, Arnie Weinmeister; E-68, Maurice Nipp; G-70, Ray Krouse.
35: BOTTOM. Washington at New York, Nov. 23, 1958. w-67, Red Stephens; w-41, Sid Watson; w-70, Ray Lemek; w-14, Eddie LeBaron; w-0, John Olszewski; d-75, Jim Katcavage; d-89, Cliff Livingston.
37: TOP. San Francisco at Baltimore, Nov. 22, 1959. w-14 (with ball), Y. A. Tittle; d-83, Don Joyce; d-89, Gino Marchetti; d-36, Bill Pellington; w-53, Frank Morze; w-79, Bob St. Clair.
BOTTOM. d-76, Gene Lipscomb; w-77, Bruce Bosley; d-52, Dick Szymanski; d-70, Art Donovan; w-14, Y. A. Tittle; w-64, Ted Connolly.
38-39: New York at Baltimore, championship game, Dec. 27, 1959. w-84, Harlan Svare; w-19, John Unitas; d-50, Madison Nutter; w-70, Sam Huff; w-76, Roosevelt Grier; w-77, Dick Modzelewski.

49: BOTTOM. Cleveland at New York, Eastern Division playoff, Dec. 21, 1958. w-86, Paul Wiggin; d-16, Frank Gifford; d-29, Alex Webster; d-42, Charlie Conerly.
52-52: San Francisco at Baltimore, Nov. 22, 1959. w-73, Leo Nomellini; w-63, Monte Clark; d-35, Alan Ameche; d-19, John Unitas; w-70, Charlie Krueger; w-55, Matt Hazeltine; d-82, Raymond Berry.
56-57: Cleveland at New York, Dec. 14, 1958. w-32, Jim Brown; w-72, Henry Jordan; w-45, Leroy Bolden; w-22, Billy Lott; d-24, Phil King; d-68, Al Barry; d-62, Bob Mischak.
60-61: Cleveland at New York, Dec. 14, 1958. d-20, Jim Patton; d-21, Carl Karilivacz; w-18, Bobby Freeman; d-76, Lou Groza.
62: Detroit at New York, Dec. 13, 1953. L-83, Jim Doran; G-86, Jim Duncan; L-22, (holding ball), Bobby Layne; L-37, Doak Walker.
63: Chicago Bears at New York, Nov. 25, 1956. w-84, Harlan Svare; w-45, Emlen Tunnell; w-25, Dick Nolan; w-48, Ed Hughes; w-20, Jim Patton; d-16, George Blanda; d-15, Ed Brown (holding ball).
62-63: Cleveland at New York, Dec. 6, 1959. w-44, Jim Shofner; w-30, Bernard Parrish; w-35, Galen Fiss; d-79, Roosevelt Brown; d-55, Ray Wietecha; d-76, Roosevelt Grier; d-88, Pat Summerall (kicking); d-42, Charlie Conerly; d-84, Harland Svare.
64-65: San Francisco at Baltimore, Nov. 22, 1959. w-73, Leo Nomellini; d-52, Dick Szymanski; w-63, Monte Clark; w-70, Charlie Krueger; d-76, Gene Lipscomb.
68: San Francisco at Baltimore, Nov. 22, 1959. w-55, Matt Hazeltine; w-40, Abe Woodson; d-82, Raymond Berry.

69: TOP. Baltimore at New York, championship game, Dec. 28, 1958. d-45, Emlen Tunnell; d-20, Jim Patton; w-84, Jim Mutscheller; d-89, Cliff Livingston.
BOTTOM. Baltimore at New York, Nov. 9, 1958. w-24, Lenny Moore.
72: Baltimore end—Jim Mutscheller.
73: Philadelphia at New York, Oct. 18, 1959. w-21, Jim Carr; d-44, Kyle Rote.
74: Los Angeles at San Francisco, Oct. 4, 1959. d-25, Dave Baker; w-24, Tom Wilson.
75: New York at Baltimore, championship game, Dec. 27, 1959. w-44, Kyle Rote; d-20, Milt Davis; d-81, Ordell Braase.
76: Detroit at New York, Dec. 13, 1953. L-25, James David; L-28, Yale Lary; G-22, Buford Long.
77: Baltimore at New York, championship game, Dec. 28, 1958. d-21, Carl Karilivacz; w-24, Lenny Moore.
78-79: Baltimore at New York, Nov. 9, 1958. w-83, Don Joyce; d-79, Roosevelt Brown; d-68, Al Barry; d-29, Alex Webster.
80-81: Los Angeles at San Francisco, Oct. 4, 1959. d-14, Y. A. Tittle; d-24, J. D. Smith; w-76, John LoVetere; d-77, Bruce Bosley; d-64, Ted Connolly; w-77, George Strugar; d-78, John Thomas.
82-83: TOP. San Francisco at Baltimore, Nov. 22, 1959. w-25, Dave Baker; d-60, George Preas; d-43, Harold Lewis; d-84, Jim Mutscheller; w-80, Jerry Mertens.
82-83: BOTTOM. New York at Baltimore, championship game, Dec. 27, 1959. Colts (d) l to r: 60, George Preas; 68, Alex Sandusky; 50, Madison Nutter; 19, John Unitas; 63, Art Spinney; 77, Jim Parker; 82, Raymond Berry. Giants (w) l to r: 75, Jim Katcavage;

77, Dick Modzelewski; 70, Sam Huff; 76, Roosevelt Grier; 20, Jim Patton; 81, Andy Robustelli; 84, Harland Svare.

84: San Francisco at Baltimore, Nov. 22, 1959. d-76, Gene Lipscomb; w-24, J. D. Smith; w-77, Bruce Bosley.

85: TOP. Leo Nomellini, San Francisco; Bill Bishop, Chicago Bears.
BOTTOM. John LoVetere, Los Angeles; Roosevelt Brown, New York.

86-87: Pittsburgh at New York, Nov. 15, 1959. w-42, Dick Alban; w-82, George Tarasovic; w-20, Jack Call; w-70, Ernie Stoutner; w-50, John Reger; d-24, Phil King.

88-89: San Francisco at Baltimore, Nov. 22, 1959. Forty-niners defense: 40, Abe Woodson; 44, Eddie Dove; 55, Matt Hazeltine; 70, Charlie Krueger; 72, Bill Herchman; 53, Frank Morze; 73, Leo Nomellini; 75, Ed Henke; 25 (rear), Dave Baker; 50, Jerry Tubbs; 80, Jerry Mertens.

90: Detroit at Chicago Bears, Dec. 13, 1959. d-50, John Damore; w-71, Alex Karras; d-79, Dick Klein; w-78, Darris McCord.

91: Taped hands of Jim Katcavage, Giants.

92-93: New York at Baltimore, championship game, Dec. 27, 1959. d-89, Gino Marchetti; w-72, Frank Youso; d-70, Art Donovan; w-55, Ray Wietecha; d-76, Gene Lipscomb; w-79, Roosevelt Brown; w-66, Jack Stroud; w-42, Charlie Conerly; d-52, Dick Szymanski.

94: Pittsburgh at New York, Dec. 5, 1954. d-70, Ernie Stoutner; w-70, Ray Krouse.

95: Baltimore at New York, championship game, December 28, 1958. w-63, Art Spinney; d-76, Roosevelt Grier.

96: Philadelphia at New York, Oct. 28, 1956. Eagle defense: 45, Rocky Ryan; 86, Norm Willey; 60, Chuck Bednarik; 75, Sid Youngelman; 52, Wayne Robinson; 78, Marion Campbell.

97: San Francisco at Baltimore, Nov. 22, 1959. d-52, linebacker Dick Szymanski; w-14, Y. A. Tittle; w-53, Frank Morze.

98: Baltimore at New York, Nov. 9, 1958. d-75, Jim Katcavage; w-45, L. G. Dupre; d-89, Cliff Livingston; w-35, Alan Ameche; d-70, Sam Huff.

99: Pittsburgh at New York, Nov. 15, 1959. d-84, Harland Svare; d-76, Roosevelt Grier; d-70, Sam Huff; w-22, Bobby Layne.

100-101: Philadelphia at New York, Oct. 18, 1959. d-70, Sam Huff; w-33, Billy Barnes.

102-103: BOTTOM. Washington at New York, Oct. 27, 1957. 20, Jim Patton.
TOP. 29, Alex Webster.
BOTTOM RIGHT. 77 Dick Modzelewski.

104: Green Bay at New York, Nov. 1, 1959. w-47, Jesse Whittenton; d-24, Phil King.

106: Detroit Lions veteran Harley Sewell, 1959.

107: New York Giants rookie Sam Huff, 1956.

108: Oct. 26, 1956. New York bench, l to r: Roosevelt Brown, Gene Filipski, Don Chandler.

109: Nov. 9, 1958, Baltimore bench, Gino Marchetti.

110: TOP. Pittsburgh at New York, Dec. 5, 1954. Steeler bench, l to r: John Schweder, Lynn Chandnois, Ernie Stoutner.

111: Oct. 16, 1955. New York bench: 31, Eddie Price; 16, Frank Gifford.

112: Dec. 13, 1953. Coach Steve Owen, New York Giants.

114: Dec. 9, 1956. New York bench, l to r: Jim Patton, Sam Huff, Emlen Tunnell; rear, Henry Moore, Bill Svoboda.

115: Roosevelt Grier.

116-117: Frank Gifford, Ray Beck, Charlie Conerly, Alex Webster.

118: Jim Katcavage, Andy Robustelli.

119: Chicago Cardinals at New York, Oct. 18, 1955.

120: July 1956, New York Giants training camp, Winooski, Vermont. Head Coach Jim Lee Howell, Offensive Coach Vince Lombardi leading drill.

Part Three

125: Baltimore Colts offensive huddle: Quarterback Unitas' head, left center.

126-127: w-19, John Unitas; d-81, Andy Robustelli; w-77, Jim Parker; w-82, Raymond Berry; d-84, Harland Svare.

128-129: w-63, Art Spinney; w-19, John Unitas; w-50, Madison Nutter; d-77, Dick Modzelewski; w-60, George Preas; d-75, Jim Katcavage; w-35, Alan Ameche.

130: d-81, Andy Robustelli; w-82, Raymond Berry; w-77, Jim Parker; w-19, John Unitas; d-70, Sam Huff; w-63, Art Spinney.

131: w-50, Madison Nutter; d-77, Dick Modzelewski; w-63, Art Spinney; w-19, John Unitas; d-72, Frank Youso; w-82, Raymond Berry; d-21, Carl Karilivacz.

132: 1. w-45, L. G. Dupre; w-35, Alan Ameche; d-75, Jim Katcavage; w-19, John Unitas.
2. d-55, Ray Wietecha; d-68, Al Barry; d-16, Frank Gifford; w-76, Gene Lipscomb; w-78, Ray Krouse.
3. w-50, Madison Nutter; w-63, Art Spinney; d-77, Dick Modzelewski; w-82, Raymond Berry; d-21, Carl Karilivacz; w-60, George Preas; d-75, Jim Katcavage.
4. w-14, George Shaw; w-65, Steve Myhra; w-76, Gene Lipscomb; w-77, Jim Parker; w-70, Art Donovan; w-83, Don Joyce; d-72, Frank Youso; d-70, Sam Huff; d-20, Jim Patton.

133: TOP. Giant co-captains Bill Svoboda, Kyle Rote, Official: Field Judge Charles Sweeney.
BOTTOM. w-23, Carl Taseff; d-42, Charlie Conerly; w-66, Don Shinnick.

134: TOP. w-19, John Unitas; Referee Ron Gibbs.

134: BOTTOM. d-20, Jim Patton; w-35, Alan Ameche; w-24, Lenny Moore; d-21, Carl Karilivacz.

135: TOP. d-77, Dick Modzelewski; d-70, Sam Huff; d-45, Emlen Tunnell; w-35, Alan Ameche.

135: BOTTOM. w-82, Raymond Berry; d-81, Andy Robustelli; d-89, Cliff Livingston; w-35, Alan Ameche; d-45, Emlen Tunnell; w-19, John Unitas.

136-137: d-73, Leo Nomellini; w-51, John Morrow; w-9, Bill Wade.

138: TOP. d-14, Y. A. Tittle; d-39, Hugh McElhenny; w-77, George Strugar; d-34, Joe Perry; d-53, Frank Morze.

139: TOP. w-48, Lex Richter; w-83, Lou Michaels; d-76, John Gonzaga; w-76, John LoVetere; d-64, Ted Connolly; d-34, Joe Perry; d-24, J. D. Smith.

138-139: d-70, Charlie Krueger; w-75, Bob Fry; w-9, Bill Wade; d-73, Leo Nomellini; w-51, John Morrow; w-79, Charlie Bradshaw; d-75, Ed Henke; d-72, Bill Herchman.

140: w-84, Leon Clarke; d-25, Dave Baker; d-50, Jerry Tubbs; d-55, Matt Hazeltine.

141: w-24, Tom Wilson; d-70, Charlie Krueger.

142: TOP. d-40, Abe Woodson; w-29, Del Shofner.

143: d-61, Bill George; w-73, Oliver Spencer.

146: TOP. d-76, John Mellekas; w-56, Joe Schmidt; w-72, Gil Mains; w-71, Alex Karras; w-78, Darris McCord; d-15, Ed Brown.

146: BOTTOM. d-60, Don Healy; w-43, Gary Lowe; w-47, Jim Martin; d-83, Bill McColl; d-78, Stan Jones; w-20, Jim Steffen.

147: TOP. d-26, Charlie Sumner; w-35, John Henry Johnson; d-81, Doug Atkins; d-31, Joe Fortunato.
BOTTOM LEFT. d-25, J. C. Caroline; w-41, Terry Barr. RIGHT. w-84, Dave Middleton.

149: d-79, Dick Klein; w-78, Darris McCord.

150-151: d-25, Dick Nolan; d-70, Sam Huff; w-32, Jimmy Brown; d-20, Jim Patton.

152: TOP LEFT. w-64, Jim Ray Smith; w-16, Milt Plum; w-56, Art Hunter; d-76, Roosevelt Grier.
BOTTOM LEFT. d-79, Roosevelt Brown; d-75, Jim Katcavage; d-74, Mike McCormack.
BOTTOM RIGHT. d-75, Jim Katcavage; w-49, Bob Mitchell.

153: w-49, Bob Mitchell; d-41, Lindon Crow; w-56, Art Hunter; d-79, Roosevelt Brown; w-32 (with ball), Jim Brown; d-89, Cliff Livingston; w-16, Milt Plum.

154: TOP. d-62, Bob Mischak; w-34, Walt Michaels; d-55, Ray Wietecha; d-66, Jack Stroud; w-73, Floyd Peters; d-33, Mel Triplett; d-16, Frank Gifford; w-44, Jim Shofner.
BOTTOM. w-24, Warren Lahr; w-44, Jim Shofner; d-16, Frank Gifford; w-22, Ken Konz; d-44, Kyle Rote; w-35, Galen Fiss.

155: w-24, Warren Lahr; d-29, Alex Webster.

157: TOP. Midweek practice, Dec. 24, 1959, New York Giants at Yankee Stadium. George Shaw left, Joe Morrison center.
BOTTOM LEFT. Defensive team meeting: Harland Svare, Jim Patton, Linden Crow, Dick Nolan, Dick Modzelewski.
BOTTOM RIGHT. Tom Landry, Defensive Coach.

158: TOP CENTER. John V. Mara, President, Giants.
TOP RIGHT. Roosevelt Grier.
CENTER RIGHT. Roosevelt Brown, Tom Landry.
BOTTOM. Don Chandler.

159: Quarterback Charlie Conerly.

160: Dick Lynch, Dick Modzelewski, Buzz Guy.

161: Offensive Coach Al Sherman, Kyle Rote, Frank Gifford.

162: TOP. w-44, Kyle Rote; d-23, Carl Taseff.

162-163: BOTTOM. d-83, Don Joyce; w-55, Ray Wietecha; w-68, Al Barry; w-44, Kyle Rote; w-42, Charlie Conerly.

167: d-19, John Unitas; d-84, Jim Mutscheller; w-81, Andy Robustelli.

168-169: w-41, Lindon Crow; d-24, Lenny Moore.

170: d-52, Dick Szymanski; d-76, Gene Lipscomb; w-29, Alex Webster; w-72, Frank Youso.

171: CENTER. d-36, Bill Pellington; w-16, Frank Gifford.
BOTTOM. d-76, Gene Lipscomb; d-23, Carl Taseff; d-89, Gino Marchetti; d-66, Don Shinnick; d-47, John Sample; w-16, Frank Gifford.

172: TOP. w-72, Frank Youso; w-66, Jack Stroud; w-33, Mel Triplett; w-42, Charlie Conerly; w-85, Bob Schnelker; d-70, Art Donovan; d-89, Gino Marchetti.
BOTTOM. w-85, Bob Schnelker; d-23, Carl Taseff; d-47, John Sample.

173: TOP. d-36, Bill Pellington; d-80, Andy Nelson; d-23, Carl Taseff; Ref. 5, Ron Gibbs.
BOTTOM. d-89, Gino Marchetti; w-29, Alex Webster; w-55, Ray Wietecha; w-42, Charlie Conerly.

175: TOP. w-25, Dick Nolan; d-84, Jim Mutscheller; w-89, Cliff Livingston.
BOTTOM. d-82, Raymond Berry; w-22, Dick Lynch; w-76, Roosevelt Grier.

182-183: d-81, Ordell Braase; d-89, Gino Marchetti; d-76, Gene Lipscomb; d-70, Art Donovan; w-16 (with ball), Frank Gifford; w-24, Phil King; w-72, Frank Youso.

184: Baltimore Colts Quarterback John Unitas.

The Tactical Changes in the Game

In completing the design of The Pros *I felt it imperative to chart clearly the transitions in offensive and defensive tactics from the postwar years to the present so that the reader might better understand and appreciate the evolution of tactical play which has made the game as brilliant as it is today. Tom Landry, the great defensive halfback and coach for the Giants, now head coach of the Dallas Cowboys, executed this progression clearly on these pages and wrote the accompanying notes.*
—ROBERT RIGER

strength over the middle. All an offensive coach would have to do to eliminate all linebackers would be to swing backs wide. (Bottom left)

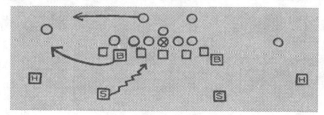

The result was that the defense lacked strength in the middle area. To alleviate this weakness coaches began to fill this area with another man. (Above)

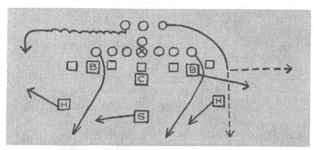

After World War II, the 5-3 defense was the major defense used. This defense was carried over from prewar years. However, it became clear by 1948 that the linebackers were being forced to cover fast halfbacks off the "T" formation. (Diagram above)

This formation, then, appeared to be the solution. However, the sweeping success of the "Split T" in college effected another major change in the early Fifties and led to the downfall of the Eagle Defense. With the introduction of the split line the middle guard found himself virtually isolated. (Below)

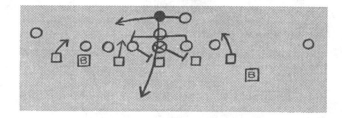

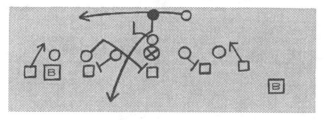

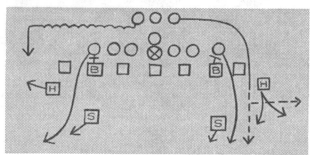

Greasy Neale, coach of the Philadelphia Eagles, came up with the idea of the "Eagle Defense," which utilized four defensive backs. With four defensive backs covering two fast halfbacks and two fast ends, the problem was solved. (Diagram above)

As the offensive play began the middle guard would "holler" for help. The only ones to help were the tackles, so they closed down on the offensive guards. Now the outside linebacker was isolated. A typical result is shown below.

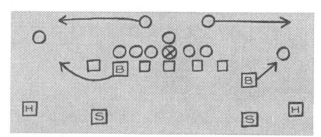

Two things happened offensively which eliminated the Eagle Defense as the most effective defense against the pro "T." First, the pass offense became very effective because of the lack of pass defensive

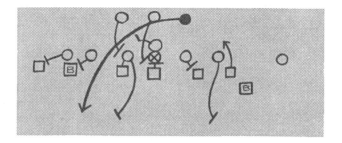

The Eagle Defense could not stop a running game with a split line. Now the defensive coaches had to turn to the only solution to their problem, a defense that would solve the two weaknesses of the Eagle Defense. The present 4-3 defense answered both needs. Here was the blending of two defenses into one: the Eagle Defense of Greasy Neale's Philadelphia team and the 6-1 "Giants Umbrella" devised by Steve Owen. The following series of diagrams show step by step the evolution of the two defenses with the 4-3 defense resulting. This should be with us for some time—the linebackers are the key.

EVOLUTION OF THE EAGLE DEFENSE BY STEPS

1. Original Eagle Defense

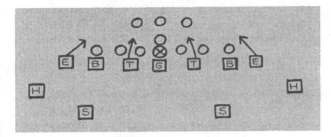

2. Countering the pass defense problem

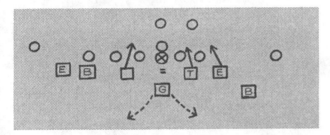

3. Tightening the tackles to help middle guard on split line

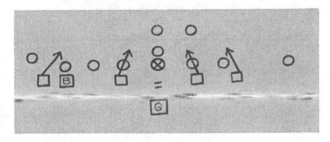

4. Putting ends inside linebackers to help them

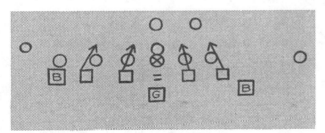

Giant coach Steve Owen picked up valuable personnel when the American Conference disbanded in 1950 and used these men to form his "Umbrella Defense," which was specifically designed to stop the new Cleveland Browns. (Above right)

EVOLUTION OF THE 6-1 UMBRELLA

1. Original 6-1 umbrella defense

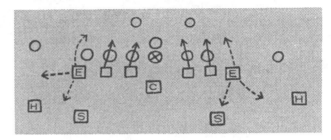

2. Switch from ends to linebackers

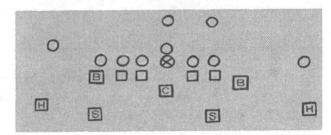

Today's 4-3 defense

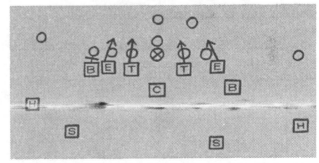

NOTE: A defense is three lines deep but is named for the front two lines. Hence a 4-3 defense is a 4-3-4 alignment.

I don't believe that there is any question of the tremendous appeal of defensive football today. Back in 1950, when Owen's famed "Umbrella Defense" stopped the powerful Cleveland Browns, 6-0, the average fan could pass this feat off as "an off-day for the Browns." Today, you can think back over the last ten years to the one constant factor in championship teams—defense! The Philadelphia Eagles of the late Forties, the Cleveland Browns of the early Fifties, the Detroit Lions of the early Fifties and the Baltimore Colts and the New York Giants of the late Fifties were all defensive powers.

The tactical changes in the game are devised by the coaches—the ingenious generals of football—and are in most cases the result of the interactions in the offensive and defensive strategies of the various teams in the league. Below are diagrams of the three key offensive changes in the last decade.

1953: In 1953 teams began using more spread formations and the slot-back was introduced to combat the 6-1 umbrella defense. This loosened the 6-1 up and gave offenses greater passing areas.

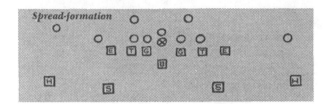

Spread-formation

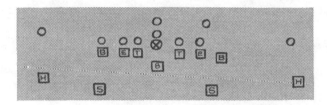

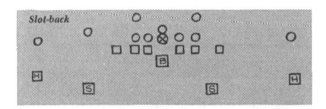

Slot-back

1956: Teams found, with the waning of the 6-1 and the more constant use of the 4-3, that they were now able to cover the spread and slot-back formations more adequately. Coaches felt, however, that offenses had to present a stronger blocking picture for the running game, and this resulted in the off-side end always spread and the end on flanker side closed for greater running strength.

1959: Al Sherman and other offensive coaches were of the opinion that teams were beginning to leave the basic 4-3 a little and play defensive men in "gaps"—to destroy stronger blocking created by the closed end and add defensive strength closest to strength of play (strong side). Perhaps offensively now there will be another trend to try to combat these "gap" defenses. (Diagram below)

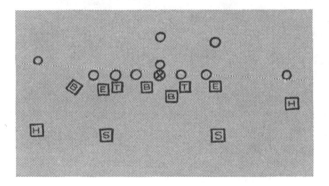

190

ACKNOWLEDGMENTS

I wish to acknowledge the great help extended to me in the preparation of this book and offer my thanks to many of those who made it possible. To the Mara family and Ray Walsh of the New York Giants for their faith in my work many years ago and their continued co-operation; to Charles Hulcher for his genius and his friendship (his sequence camera was used for many of the pictures in this book); to my dear wife, Eleanor, a great pro football fan, who patiently insisted I publish my football photographs as a book and then gave untiring help in its completion; to Peter Schwed and Dick Grossman, my editors at Simon and Schuster, who gave me encouragement and room to roam in a new field—the photographic book.

To the clubs in the National Football League who so generously supplied historical material and loaned their rare old films; to the Stiller Company in Green Bay; and to Peter Sansone and United Press International for their matchless old-time picture source.

A tribute to Eastman Kodak, whose Tri-X film is so remarkable and consistent as to withstand all the demands I put to it under all conditions of light and weather; to the Corvelle brothers at Towne Laboratories for their long and faithful service; to Fred Roe for his invaluable darkroom help; and to George Emanuel and the entire staff at Finley Photographic, New York.

R.R.

BOB WATERFIELD WORKS THE BOOTLEG PLAY

SID LUCKMAN AND BULLDOG TURNER

SAMMY BAUGH

JIM THORPE

RED GRANGE RUNS THE PASS OPTION

Printed in the United States
By Bookmasters